Morning Star

A Moravian star. *(Photograph by Cookie Snyder. Courtesy of* The Winston-Salem Journal, *by permission of William E. East.)*

Morning Star

The Life and Works
of
Francis Florentine Hagen
(1815–1907)
Moravian Evangelist and Composer

James Boeringer

The Moravian Music Foundation Press
Winston-Salem, North Carolina
Bethlehem, Pennsylvania
London and Toronto: Associated University Presses

© 1986 by Associated University Presses, Inc.

Associated University Presses
440 Forsgate Drive
Cranbury, NJ 08512

Associated University Presses
25 Sicilian Avenue
London WC1A 2QH, England

Associated University Presses
2133 Royal Windsor Drive
Unit 1
Mississauga, Ontario
Canada L5J 1K5

Library of Congress Cataloging in Publication Data

Boeringer, James.
  Morning star.

  Bibliography: p.
  "Musical compositions of Francis Florentine Hagen": p.
  1. Hagen, Francis Florentine, 1815–1907.
2. Composers—United States—Biography.   I. Title.
ML410.H145B6   1985   783'.092'4 [B]   84-62100
ISBN 0-941642-01-1

Printed in the United States of America

*This book is dedicated to all of the
Morning Star Soloists
since Christmas Eve 1836*

Both the shepherds and the seers . . . at the end of their road . . .
found a shining Child and an unquenchable Star.

Winifred Kirkland

I, Jesus, have sent mine angel to testify unto you these things in
the churches: I am the Root and Offspring of David, the bright
and Morning Star.

The Revelation of St. John the Divine

Contents

Illustrations

N.B. This book also contains numerous musical and music-related facsimiles.

Acknowledgments

I express my gratitude to Elizabeth Hagen Pfaff, granddaughter of the composer, who provided primary sources, valuable hints, and family remembrances. She and her husband, Frederick Wilson Pfaff, also supplied me with constant kind encouragement and material support without which the book would not have been written.

Moravian archivists Vernon Nelson (North) and Mary Creech (South) were most cooperative in placing at my disposal the documents in their keeping. Researcher Robert Steelman of Moravian College functioned as my northern emissary, searching out biographical details and elusive bibliographical items.

The second version of the actual text was written in the mountain cabin of my mother, Mildred Boeringer, to whom I express my gratitude for the unlimited space, coffee, and seclusion that she provided.

I am also grateful to Dr. Dale Gramley and the Rev. Henry Williams, members of the Moravian Music Foundation Press Board, for their many helpful and expert suggestions.

I express my thanks to Mrs. Irene Beroth Wooten, who meticulously typed each version of the text with great care, patiently accepting, after each rewriting, the tattered remnants of her earlier flawless work; to Mrs. Mitzie Kimball, who dealt with repeated deletions, insertions, and rearrangements, patiently carrying out my requests even when I brought new versions back to her, saying that I had decided the first way was better after all; and to Wes Stewart of the Museum of Early Southern Decorative Arts, who copied many of the photographs. Staff members of Old Salem, Inc., particularly Frances Griffin, were also most helpful.

Unless otherwise indicated, all illustrations and examples reproduced in this volume are from originals owned by the Moravian Music Foundation.

Chronology

Dates at the far left apply to events in Hagen's life; dates that are indented apply to his musical compositions, the numbers for which (see Appendix 3) are provided at the far right.

1815 born in Salem
1826 to Nazareth as student

1834	"Schlaf, liebes Kind"	60
1834	"Sel'ge Lebensstunden"	61

1835 to Salem as a teacher

5 February 1836	"O delightful theme"	49
24 December 1836	"Morning Star"	44; see Appendix 1

1837 to Nazareth as teacher

ca. 1838	*Scherzo capriccioso*	59
ca. 1839?	"Remembrance" Rondoletto	54
ca. 1840	"Herr wie sind deine Werke so gross und viel"	29

1841 marriage and conversion

Ante 1843	*The Lay of the Troubadour*	71
Before 1844(1836?)	Overture in F Major	51
Before 1844	"Bis dereinst mein Stündlein schlägt"	14

1844 ordained Deacon, to Bethania as pastor
1851 ordained Presbyter; to Friedland and Mt. Bethel as pastor
1852 to Friedberg as pastor

October 1853	"Ye are come unto Mount Zion"	80

1854 to York as pastor

1854	*Alma mater*	5

1861 to Bethlehem, member of P.E.C.
1862 widowed
1864 second marriage

1866	*The Grave of My Wife*	68

1867 to New Dorp, Staten Island; visit to Herrnhut
1870 to New York City as missionary
1872 widowed again
1875 to Iowa
1877 retired

1878 to Bethlehem as retiree

1 August 1878	"Praise waiteth for thee"	53
31 August 1878	"How amiable are thy tabernacles"	31
12 June 1879	"Unto the Lamb"	74
January 1880	"And the seventh angel"	8

1880 to Philadelphia

September 1880–June 1882 *Organist's Companion*

1882 to Tremont, New York; later, to Philadelphia

1882	"A loving home"	2
1882	"Am I a soldier"	6
1882	*Christmas Bells*	18
1883	"A friend in need"	1
ca. 1884	"What good news the angels bring"	79

1884 to Bethlehem

1886 to Salem (earthquake and revival)

1887 to Philadelphia

1887	"Mowing the harvest hay"	45

1888 temporarily to Easton as pastor, then back to Philadelphia

1891	*Christmas Cantata*	19

1895 to York with Ernest

November 1898	"Lob, Preis und Dank"	39
November 1898	"Nun lege ich mich schlafen"	48

1902 to Lititz with Ernest

1907 died in Lititz

Morning Star

"Morning Star." First edition, 1857, cover and first two pages of the music.
The publication continues with two more pages containing identical music,
but with stanzas 3 and 4 of the text of ante 1857, q.v. in Appendix 1.

THE MORNING STAR.

THE ENGLISH WORDS BY
THE REV: M. HOUSER.

THE MUSIC BY
THE REV: F. F. HAGEN.

Soprano. Alto.

SOLO.

1. Morning star thy cheer-ing light Can dis-pel the gloom of
Morgen stern auf fin — stre Nacht Der die Welt - voll Freu de

Tenor. Basso.

2. Thine ef - ful-gence glo-rious light Far ex - ceeds the sun so
Dei - nes Glan - zes her - lich - keit Ue — ber trifft die Son - ne

CHORUS.

night Morning star thy cheer-ing light Can dis-pel the gloom of
nacht Morgen stern auf fin - stre Nacht Der die Welt voll Freu de

bright Thine ef - ful-gence glo -rious light Far ex - ceeds the sun so
welt: Dei - nes Glan - zes her - lich - keit Ue — ber trifft die Son - ne

SOLO.   CHORUS.   SOLO.   CHORUS.

night Light di - vine   come and shine   come and shine   Light di-
nacht Je - su - lein   komm her - ein   komm her - ein   Je - su-

bright Je - sus thou   canst be - stow,   Je - sus thou   canst be-
welt Du al - lein   Je - su - lein!   Je - su - lein!   Du al-

cres.   f

-vine, In this dark - - some   heart   of   mine:
-lein, leucht' in mei - - nes   Her - - zens   Schrein.

-stow More than thou - - sand   suns   can   do:
-lein, Bist was tau - - send   Son - - nen   sein.

cres.

1
Morning Star

Francis Florentine Hagen (1815–1907) was a minister of the Unitas Fratrum, a Protestant denomination established by followers of John Huss in 1457. Persecution nearly extirpated the group by 1722, but in that year the survivors found refuge in Saxony on the estate of Count Ludwig von Zinzendorf. There they built a town called Herrnhut and experienced a renewal and revival that shaped what is now called the Moravian Church.

During the early years of their renewal, the Brethren came to be called Moravians and developed individualistic traditions of life and worship, one of which is the lovefeast, a musical service during which a simple meal is served to mark some special event. Christmas is one such event, and the lovefeast that celebrates it touches all the senses.

When you walk into an American Moravian church, you see evergreen swags and a large white paper star, internally illuminated, hanging over the pulpit. An usher hands you a printed ode that contains the texts of the hymns and anthems to be sung. While you sing the hymns, dieners (servers) come to the ends of the pews with baskets of aromatic buns and trays of mugs filled with sweet, milky coffee. You help to pass the buns and mugs along your row, and after grace is sung, you enjoy your little meal while the choir sings for you.

One of the anthems is "Morning Star," sung antiphonally by

a child soloist and the choir. It has an ingenuous text about Jesus, who, according to Saint John the Divine, called himself the Morning Star. The music to which the anthem is traditionally sung in America is a simple sixteen-measure carol that was composed by Hagen. It is the best known of his compositions, and it may be the best known of all the thousands of choral-instrumental works that Moravian composers have produced.

Each Christmas more children in Moravian churches all over North America know the thrill of being the Morning Star soloist at a lovefeast, ever since the first performance of the piece was given on Christmas Eve, 1836, in Salem, North Carolina. Each Christmas hundreds of grown-up children in responding choirs and listening congregations remember and relive that same experience of their childhood.

The little song bears heavy symbolic freight: it stands for the childlike Hagen; for the children of the Moravian church, to whom he dedicated it; for the child in each of us that Christmas sentiment evokes; and finally for the Child who was the incarnate Morning Star.

The song symbolizes all those things more meaningfully and beautifully than some great and impressive piece of music for the same reason that Jesus, when his disciples asked who was the greatest in the Kingdom of Heaven, called a little child and set him in the midst of them.

Hagen has, in effect, done the same thing.

"Morning Star" is one of eighty-one works that Hagen composed between 1834 and 1898, and music was only one of many activities in which he involved himself. He composed choral, keyboard, and instrumental music; and besides being a composer and performer, he was a teacher, preacher, and evangelist in the church, and an editor, translator, and writer in the fields of history and religion. The variety of his pursuits makes biographical synthesis difficult, because the biographer feels, as it were, outnumbered.

Hagen had no time for speciousness, but always found time for what he called *edification*. His memory was retentive throughout his long life, and he was insatiably curious and continuously productive. His grandson, John F. Hagen, says in "Memories" that his grandfather "understood six languages and was conversant in four. . . . He was an excellent writer, and his racy style seems almost modern." Words and music must have coursed constantly through Francis Hagen's brilliant mind, and the papers that he left reveal the full sweep of his powerful and many-faceted personality.

The first category of these papers upon which this book is based is Hagen's diaries. He wrote on 21 December 1877 to E. T. Kluge, then editor of the *Moravian:*

> I have no special fondness, and still less talent, for keeping a diary. I moreover confess to some nervousness on the subject, ever since I learnt that some people call a diary a fool's mirror. But . . . there may be some good in diaries, as in everything else.

Five of his personal diaries survive (earliest, 1838; latest, 1880s), and to these can be added an early memorandum book and the church diaries that were kept by all Moravian ministers. All diary quotations in this book are cited by date. Those that are ecclesiastical were partly printed in *Records*, and for those citations the page numbers are also provided.

Each Moravian in the old days wrote a *Lebenslauf (Memoir)*, a chronicle of spiritual development that also contained a certain amount of biographical information. When the writer died, the document was completed by the pastor or a friend and was read at the funeral. Hagen wrote his own *Lebenslauf* in German in about 1860. Each extract from this second source used in this book is headed *Memoir.*

In addition, Hagen wrote an *Auto-Biography* in English in 1901. It survives in two similar versions that I have combined as my third source, quotations from which are headed *Auto-Biography.*

Hagen was, like most Moravians, very conscious of the passage of time, marking anniversaries faithfully. His birthday book, still kept up by the family, is my fourth source. In his diaries, Hagen frequently took stock of his life on his own birthday and on New Year's Eve.

My fifth and final source is Hagen's accumulation of, and commentary upon, what he called Moravian *lore.* The earliest records of Moravian communities and congregations were summarized in handwritten *Nachrichten* that were circulated among the centers of activity. Later these developed into periodicals. Since American Moravian settlements were controlled as missionary outposts from Herrnhut until 1857, the continual *Brüder-Blatt* was the first standard church periodical in this country. In 1822, however, the Moravians here had also initiated the *Missionary Intelligencer,* followed in 1850 by the *Moravian Church Miscellany.*

The *Moravian* was established by an 1855 act of Synod, whereby the "brother who was elected Editor [Edmund de Schweinitz] . . . received . . .'power to call to his aid the service of such persons as he might deem proper.'" De Schweinitz interpreted this authorization to mean that he could appoint co-editors, and he did so, choosing Hagen and Rev. Lewis F. Kampmann and calling them "in every respect co-editors of the *Moravian*, all three equally responsible to Synod."

Hagen's industriousness and his love of words made him an excellent choice. Seeking just the right translation for the German word *Sünderschaft*, for example, he was inspired to invent *sinnership*, which is precisely right. "Church patriotism" was an expression used by nineteenth-century Moravians. Hagen himself used it at least once but later wrote to the *Moravian* to call it a solecism serving "as a beautiful ecclesiastical cloak for mere sectarianism [or] . . . denominationalism." Hagen said that people consider those terms "suggestive of bigotry, exclusivism, and intolerance, whereas patriotism has a good sound. And sound, we know, sometimes passes for sense." He continues,

> I have nothing to say against a proper reverence for the history, traditions, and forms of one's own denomination, . . . but I think we ought to call things by their right names. I prefer the expression "lore" to "patriotism." It sounds quite as well, and is not in any respect absurd.

Hagen steeped himself in Moravian lore, and his doing so shaped his personality and his career. He believed that the way Moravians had thought and lived and worked in the early years of their renewal was not only a viable way of life but also the best, or perhaps the only, way. All of the words and music that poured constantly out of him were calculated to transmit to others the religious experiences that had changed and vitalized his own life. He was an evangelist not only in the pulpit but in almost everything he wrote, whether it was verbal or musical.

At the end of his life, Hagen could no longer write, and he could hardly see or hear. His granddaughter Mary Hagen Mills tells us that

> A pastime he thoroughly enjoyed was cutting pictures from the newspapers and pasting them into stiff-cover blank books. There was a large bookcase of those books when he died. Of course he did most of the cutting and pasting in by feeling. After the pictures were pasted into the book, if any stuck out over the edges, he just trimmed them off, regardless of how much or little remained of the pictures.

Though he could not see what he was doing, and the activity of his fingers was meaningless, his clear mind and reliable memory were still active, and Mrs. Mills remembers also

> how he used to pass much of his time by repeating aloud scrip-
> ture passages and by singing hymns both in English and in Ger-
> man.

Thus he had his words and music to the very end; and his last stanza was, according to his obituary,

> Mein Gott, ich bitt' durch Christi blut,
> Mach Du's mit meinem Ende gut.
>
> (My Lord, I pray, by Jesus' blood,
> Do make my final day be good.)

The same document tells us that at his funeral,

> The choir sang "Morning Star" . . . , Miss Emily Miksch singing
> the solo.

Francis Florentine Hagen as a child. So far as is now known, this is the first publication of this silhouette, which was probably cut in about 1830.

2
Child

Auto-Biography

Five children were born, of whom I was the first.

*H*agen's whole life was filled with children. When he was himself a child, they were his siblings and schoolmates. When he became a teacher, they were his students. They were twice his very own, for he married twice and fathered two families. Late in his life they were his grandchildren. Now they are the Morning Star Soloists, a constantly enlarging host. In both his *Memoir* and *Auto-Biography*, Hagen refers to children with striking frequency.

Hagen's first known compositions, "Schlaf, liebes Kind" (no. 60) and "Sel'ge Lebensstunden" (no. 61), both composed in 1834, and his last two, "Lob, Preis und Dank" (no. 39) and "Nun lege ich mich schlafen" (no. 48), both composed in November 1898, are all directed to children. Sixty-four years separate these two pairs of works, but the same childlike spirit suffuses all of them. Between these compositions come other works for or about children, in addition to "Morning Star," such as "Hail, thou wondrous infant Stranger" (no. 27); "What good news the angels bring" (no. 79), which is an antiphonal work for adult and "juvenile" choir; and his longest work,

Christmas Cantata (no. 19; partly lost), composed for a Sunday school.

Children were Hagen's best-loved people, and Salem, North Carolina, was his best-loved place. Winifred Kirkland may have expressed the reason why, for she connects the two:

> The only way to visit old Salem . . . is with a child's heart for luggage. . . . Unless you have learned the wisdom that knows how to put away grown-up things, you cannot really enter the Christmas City.

Auto-Biography

I was born at Salem, North Carolina, on the 30th of October 1815.

Hagen lived in many different places, but his heart was always in Salem, where he attended the Boys' School from age five until he was about eleven (1820–1826). Then he went to Mora-

Salem, North Carolina. This was the Moravian community in which Hagen was born. Painting by Daniel Welfare (1824), depicting Salem from the southwest. *(Courtesy of Wachovia Historical Society, by permission of Dale H. Gramley. Photograph courtesy of Old Salem, Inc., by permission of Robert L. Stern.)*

vian schools in Pennsylvania until he was about twenty (1826–1835), returning to Salem to teach at the Academy for two years (1835–1837). After that he taught at Nazareth Hall for seven years (1837–1844), coming back to Salem once again (1841) to get married to his first wife, Clara.

After he was ordained a Deacon of the Moravian Church in 1844, Hagen spent the next ten years serving churches that were so near to Salem as to have seemed like home to him: Bethania and Bethabara (1844–1851); Friedland and Mt. Bethel, Virginia (1851–1852); and Friedberg (1852–1854), with some simultaneous duties in nearby Pfafftown.

He spent 1854 to 1861 in York, where he conducted revivals that were not entirely popular with his congregation, and 1861 to 1867 in Bethlehem as a member of the P.E.C. In 1862 Hagen was widowed for the first time and in 1864 he brought his second wife from York. One might say that Hagen spent his middle years from 30 May 1862 (when Clara died) to 1886 (when he moved to Salem) engaged in an increasingly difficult struggle to bring up the young children of his second marriage. From that time on, his tenures in any one town were brief: New Dorp 1867–1870, during which he was a delegate to the 1869 General Synod in Herrnhut; Brooklyn, New York, 1870–1875; and Iowa, 1875–1878. Then he retired, but he provided service to Bethlehem 1878–1880; Philadelphia, 1880–1882; Tremont, New York, 1882; Philadelphia, 1882–1884; and finally Bethlehem, 1884–1886.

He made his last visit to Salem in 1886 to 1887, and the three last cities in which he lived, all in Pennsylvania, were Philadelphia, 1887–1895; York, 1895–1902; and Lititz, March 1902 until his death 7 July 1907 at the age of ninety-one years, eight months, and seven days.

Auto-Biography

My father was John Joachim Hagen and my sainted mother Susanna Lick Hagen. My father had spent the best part of his adult years as an assistant missionary from the Moravian Church at Herrnhut, Saxony, to the Indians in Canada and Ohio. When disabled by malarial disease, he returned, a cripple for life, and [was] called to Salem N.C. as Schneider Meister (master tailor) of that place. . . . His native home was Polkern (Bolkern) in the Altemark, Prussia, Europe.

Johann Joachim had been born in 1771 and had worked as a blacksmith, emigrating to North America in 1804. When he left the mission field, he went first to Lititz and from there to Salem, when his arrival (9 April 1814) was noted as follows (R, p. 3225).

His intention is to visit here, and to see whether he can establish himself as a tailor. This will suit well in the Brothers House and he will be able to find sufficient work.

By November 1814 (R, p. 3241) he was applying "to settle as a citizen," and to rent the then empty home of Br. and Sr. Byhan.

His tailoring goes well, and he has some means of his own; also in view of his service as a missionary and his lameness resulting therefrom he can count on assistance from the Mission diaconie if he needs it.

Auto-Biography

My father soon found an excellent help-mate in the Sister's

Johann Joachim Hagen's house. Hagen was born here in 1815. The house still stands on Salt Street in Old Salem. *(Photograph courtesy of Old Salem, Inc., by permission of Robert L. Stern.)*

home, & they, having married "in the Lord", founded a happy & prosperous home. They were both poor in worldly goods, but, rich in faith, they found contentment to be great gain.

The "help-mate" to whom Hagen refers was Susanna Lick (born 23 November 1787, Salem, North Carolina and died 23 June 1853, Salem, North Carolina). Johann Joachim had begun preparing for married life by applying on 2 August 1814 (*R*, p. 3241) for the Salem building lot south of Br. Bagge, but he did not receive it. He was betrothed to Sr. Susanna on 18 December 1814 (*R*, p. 3242, under the date 20 December). The marriage took place on 26 December 1814, Johann Joachim then being 43 years old and Susanna 27. The couple had five children, Franz Florentin, Louise Cynthia, Ernest Julius, Augusta Maria, and Johanetta Florentina.

Memoir

In holy baptism I was dedicated forever as belonging to the Lord—and how wonderfully has our faithful God maintained that bond and compassion and always inspired a thirst for righteousness! My beloved parents had intended me from the beginning for the Lord and his service, and how many prayers they sent up on behalf of their first born is known only to him from whom no secrets are hid. I was taught about the Saviour from an early age, and prayers to the children's Friend were emphasized, and often, since I shirked my evening prayers, I had rather a lot to do.

Johann Joachim and Susanna were excellent parents and providers, and Francis's youth was evidently very happy.

Auto-Biography

My parents above all things desired to give their children a good Christian education, a better legacy by far than earthly riches. Our excellent Moravian schools greatly favored their wishes. My father . . . labored with remarkable industry to supply the needful means to the above end.

The Moravian schools were very good, indeed. Their high quality dated back to the earliest days. Wesley's Journal (*Landmarks*, p. 89) tells us that in 1738 in Herrnhut, Latin, Greek, Hebrew, French, and English were all taught, along with the three R's, history, and geography. Prayer and walking were

The Old Salem Academy building. This is the cover of Hagen's song *Alma mater* (no. 5), published in 1854 when the old Salem Academy building, which had been constructed in 1771, was torn down.

distributed throughout the day, as well as singing and expounding the scriptures.

The 1733 *Extract of the Constitution* (*Landmarks*, p. 95) tells us that each day contained five hours of sleep (11 P.M. to 4 A.M.), three hours for eating and for spiritual sustenance, and fourteen hours of work. There were services twice daily, at 8:00 A.M. and at 8:00 P.M.

Francis Hagen was a student about a century after the time described, but the discipline in his school days was as good, and the curriculum was as nourishing. Non-Moravians were not permitted to own property in the settlements, but the schools accepted non-Moravian students. Outsiders were eager to enroll their children, because no better education was available anywhere in North America. Here are some of Hagen's remembrances of his school days.

Memoir

When I was five years old, I started school, and the Lord, who had heard my childish pleas, gave me the needful intelligence and understanding, and love and determination, to learn, even though I often betrayed my Saviour through my laziness, irreverence, and daydreaming. In the earliest years of my schooling, the Spirit of God worked in my heart in a blessed way, making impressions upon me that became guardian angels that were always at hand in later years, when I was buffeted this way and that by the freshets of sin, perpetually helping me to cling tightly to the Friend of sinners, even when I was far away.

Still deeply engraved on my memory are the closing assemblies of the Children's Festivals, at which, full of rue at my sins, I would draw away from the other children and beg forgiveness for my sins. But, oh! sin grew stronger as I grew older; my heart was evil; and the detrimental influence of bad companions little by little led me more and more distant from my dedication to God, until finally I fell under almost the same condemnation, and slipped more and more deeply into sin.

Anything less than total devotion to Jesus was sin to Hagen, so that what would have been mere bagatelles to others seemed enormities to him. He was later to be ashamed of loving music; of allowing his mind to wander during meditation and prayer; and of feeling inconsolable grief at the untimely death of one of his young children. He was, in point of fact, merely being human. Though he judged himself severely for such responses, he was deeply sympathetic with those who suffered and responded as he himself did. He writes in his Blairstown diary, 29 and 30 October 1877,

Mr. Franzmann, a neighbor 1 mile east of Blairstown, came [Monday] to announce the death of his oldest daughter (12) of diphtheria & engage my service at the funeral. This morning [Tuesday] another daughter of the above Franzman, aged 5, died October 1877 of the disease. In the afternoon I visited them & found the mother & 3 children sick abed of the same. . . . The funeral of Mr. Franzmann's two children took place at 1 p.m. Wednesday . . . in the German & English language. The mother & three children lay sick, very sick, of diphtheria in another room. It was heartrending to behold the poor mother totter to the coffin of her two daughters to take a farewell view of their loved faces. . . . Many a silent prayer went up that this may prove the turning point in the life of this afflicted family.

We of later times accuse those who lived in the nineteenth century of sentimentality and exaggeration, but we forget how ubiquitous sickness, pain, and death were in those days. Ministers of our day seldom have to conduct funerals of children, but Hagen carried out such duties every week. Parents and grandparents had for consolation only the promises of Jesus and the sentiments of the arts, and the latter seemed exaggerated to us now only because we have less need of them.

Hagen was a man of the nineteenth century, having missed only the first fifteen years of it. He loved children with a special intensity because they perished so easily and so frequently, and because he, too, was a child at heart. On 30 October 1879, he wrote in his diary,

Birthday. 64. Supped with kind Br. Rondthaler. Letters from children, viz., Sam^1. Willie, Ernest & f^r S^m Augusta, Louise & her husb. But none from the others. Parents love children more than children do parents, & so it was with those who are now parents, when they were children. Yet children may & do love their parents more than they show, God bless them.

Hagen was thus capable of being both vulnerable and cranky, but he never lost his capacity for childlike inquisitiveness, wonder, puckishness, and whimsy. His grandson, John Francis Hagen, substantiates this inference in his "Memories":

These memories of my grandfather cover those years of my youth from six to seventeen. [He] was a delight to all children. He had a way with them. In any group he first made the acquaintance of the children no matter how important the adults. He had a sly way of slipping nickles, dimes, and quarters to youngsters, somewhat in keeping with their age.

The warmth of Hagen's grandson's memories permeates his charming essay. He continues,

> Railway travel excited him, and he insisted on arriving at the station a full hour before train departure.

When it came time at the age of seventy-one for Hagen to return to the town where he had been a boy, he began to get ready a month ahead of time, and we can sense in his diary entries the high anticipation he felt:

> [7 January 1886 in Bethlehem] "I am preparing to move to Salem N. C." [1 March 1886] "Busy packing up." [4 March 1886] "Sent off goods to Salem N. C. & started for Philad[a] at 8:40 a.m." [5 March 1886] "Left Philad[a] at 12:05 p.m. for Washington with Harry. Were present at the sessions of the Senate & House of Representatives. Saw White House, Harry indignant at the occupant. Left Washington at 11 p.m.; reached Danville V[a] next morning [6 March 1886] at 7 & Greensboro at 9 and Salem at 12, where we took up our quarters at Mrs. Crosland's, who lives on the very lot on which my father's house stood when I was born Oct. 30, 1815. From my west window I can see the old homestead on Salt Street where I was born. We are quite comfortable, but very weary." [11 March 1886] "My goods arrived." [22 March 1886] "My new table came." [13 May 1886] "My books arrived from Beth[m] yesterday."

Finally he had all his belongings together in Salem, and he enjoyed himself enormously, preaching at many of the churches that he had served about forty years before.

Hagen also always had a childlike and comprehensive curiosity about scientific phenomena. While still recovering from a stroke in Philadelphia (5 December 1882), he noted, "Transit of Venus fr. 9 a.m. to 3 p.m." On 6 December 1886 he wrote, "On Friday night 9 o'clock the moon had a large ring around it," and on 19 January 1887, "At my request Prof. Wurreschke and class measured one of the grand sycamores in the Square and found it to be 109 feet high!"

New Year's Eve was always a time of important retrospective contemplation for Hagen, and it was particularly so in 1886 in his boyhood home:

> Am sitting alone in my room, while Salem Cong. is spending an hour in hearing the Memorabilia of the closing year, &c. I, too, look back upon the past and up to heaven and feel
> 1. thankful for the past, for the Lord having permitted me to return to my native town & to live on the very lot on which I was

born & in sight of the old homestead on Salt St. where I was reared; he has kept me safely hitherto & once more permitted me to see—both in my native town & in the congregations around where I had been stationed as pastor for about 11 year (reckoning fr. Sept. 22, 1844)—some glorious revivals of religion;

2dly confid ent that the Lord who has been with me for the last 72 years, dating fr. Oct. 30, 1815, will lead me all my journeys through; &

3dly hopeful that if my earthly career shall end during the New Year, he will accept me & in their turn my beloved children through blood-bought grace. Amen.

3
Single Brother

*H*agen's twelfth through twenty-sixth years—the time while
he was a Single Brother, i.e., a bachelor—were as difficult
for him as they are for most people. He oscillated widely between letting his high spirits and sense of humor take over, and
cultivating the sobriety and contemplative righteousness that
he desired. He spent most of these years, 1826 to 1841, in
Nazareth, first as a student and later as a teacher, with a brief
interlude back in Salem, also as a teacher.

Auto-Biography

. . . After enjoying the advantages of our parochial school at
Salem, I was sent in my twelfth year as a "gratuitous" to
Nazareth Hall Boarding School then under the direction of Rev.
J. G. Herman, Principal Jeremiad at Nazareth, as a student in the
preparation class, & then entered the Theological Seminary.

Nazareth had mothered Bethlehem in much the same way as
Bethabara had mothered Salem. In Hagen's day, Nazareth was
the home of the leading northern Moravian boys' school, and
the Moravian Theological Seminary was still located there. Very
few southerners attended Nazareth Hall; between its founding
in 1785 and Hagen's graduation in 1829, only 27 of its 648

Francis Florentine Hagen as a student. John Francis Hagen, in "Some memories . . . ," describes his grandfather thus: "Grandfather was tall, erect, imposing. This was further emphasized by a 'topper' which he . . . utilized to carry papers."

students had come from towns south of Baltimore. Having absorbed the best that Salem schools could offer, Hagen was about to be exposed to the disciplines and challenges of Nazareth.

Memoir

Meanwhile, in my twelfth year, I was sent to Nazareth Hall in order to further my studies there, and to prepare myself for serving the Lord in the congregations. The training lavished on me, and the incomparable opportunities that were available to me in this beautiful institution—these alone, nevertheless, did not serve to help me to reach my desired goal, for my heart was not in it. My willing confirmation in this year made an impression upon me, and I approached the holy Supper for the first time with great sincerity, but there was little in my head, and nothing in my heart, but only a certain intimidation by the holy sacrament, without truly heartfelt satisfaction. Here I give a thousand thanks for the mercy of the Saviour, that he nevertheless bore with me so patiently and did not rest until he had opened my eyes, that I might myself make manifest his great love for sinners.

Hagen was an eager and responsive student, an ideal subject to receive all of the varied manifestations of Moravian faith, life, and culture. He was quick with languages, adding Latin, Greek, and French to his German-English bilinguality. He had perfect pitch, and had become a pianist by the age of twelve. He had quickly learned to play several other instruments, especially the violin, and soon developed an aptness for musical composition. He was socially gregarious, intellectually curious, and artistically creative. As the son of a missionary, he was deeply religious. John F. Hagen tells us of his grandfather in his "Memories,"

His love of music began in his early years. He played the pipe-organ at the age of twelve and at maturity was skillful with most musical instruments. It is believed that the violin was his favorite.

Auto-Biography

Having finished my course, I was sent back to Salem N. C. as teacher in the Boys' Parochial School, in which I had once been a pupil, and which was then under the able direction of Bishop

John C. Bechler, a noted scholar & excellent composer.

Memoir

In my [20th] year, at the end of my studies, I left the Nazareth Seminary in obedience to a call to teach in Salem. How little did I, at that time, deserve such an important position, how insufficiently enlightened I was, in view of my character at that time! Separated from God, without love for the Saviour (without which we can do nothing), full of desire and love for sin that was ruling me ever more strongly and whose willing servant I had already been for a long time: yea, I was so much without true love for the more significant occupations, for the usual affections to which even ignorant children of the world are inclined, that during this time I was like a reed blown hither and thither by the wind, and was thus ill suited to be useful by word or example to the students in my keeping.

Besides my especially strong inclination to sin, and all sorts of worldly activities, I exercised extensively my love of music, which was for me still an unconsecrated art, to my great disadvantage. I dedicated my best time to music, and put it before everything else, thereby putting something subsidiary in place of more substantial and useful skills, and in preparation, especially, for a blessed hereafter.

Hagen was born a century too late. It was typical of early Moravian composers, such as Antes and J. F. Peter, to feel guilty about their desire to write and perform absolute music, but Hagen is the only later Moravian composer who believed that music could lead to sin. That is not to say that he was a Puritan: he was quite capable of being naughty and of laughing at his own naughtiness and that of others. One of his escapades came to the attention of the Salem Aufseher Collegium 22 August 1836 (*R*, p. 4227).

It was brought up that some time ago a Mr. Murbach and others serenaded the Square until toward midnight and the neighbors complained that they had been disturbed. As pleasant as this serenading is for many members, it was the wish of Auf. Col. that in the future it should not be continued until late in the night, since many disorders can grow out of this, as was recently the case in the tavern, where several single Brehtren—Wm. Leinbach, Francis Hagen, Eph. Brietz, and Aug. Zevely—loitered until 11 o'clock and created disorder. Auf. Col. finds it necessary that Br. Schulz speak with Br. Schaaf about these Brethren.

A letter (27 December 1966) from Hagen's grandson, John

Francis Hagen, to former Foundation Director Ewald F. Nolte, describes the event and connects it with a musical composition.

> They were rebuked by the Moravian minister. Grandfather returned home and, smarting from the severe rebuke, wrote his secular in F major.

John Francis implies that this was Hagen's overture (no. 51), which was dedicated to the Bethlehem Philharmonic. Rau & David, p. 114, substantiates that the overture was early, dating it before 1844. It we accept John Francis' hint, the work was actually composed in 1836, and Hagen would have taken the work north with him the following year and added the dedication. Some other work may have been involved. Moravians sometimes composed secular music with guilty surreptitiousness, but this may be the only instance of a Moravian work conceived in defiance.

Nevertheless, Hagen's sense of his own sinfulness was terrible to him, as in this description of his agony written in his diary of 1838.

> There was a great snowstorm in the afternoon, which continued to increase in the evening. After dinner, I conceived the idea to make another attempt to recover myself from my back-slidden state. . . . To this end I betook myself to the vestry room (S.E. corner of second floor of Nazareth Hall, west of the teachers room), in which the ministers robed themselves for Communion & where the sacred utensils and gowns, &c., &c., were kept, &

Nazareth Hall.

the walls of which were lined with old paintings of passion scenes, portraits, &c., &c. I gave myself over to meditations, which I reduced to writing on the spot. . . .

The following were my reflections at this moment: I have hitherto led a wicked life & I now earnestly desire to be connected and reconciled to God. I wish to love him warmly, but I find it no easy matter. . . . I am of a sanguine disposition & that whatever interests me most is constantly present to my thoughts. I also know that my God ought to be uppermost in my thoughts & that, if I ever loved God at all, I would love him much & then (O bliss!) much would be forgiven (Luke 7:47). The question now arises, "How can this love be produced within me?"

. . .Were I a new man, quite regenerated & more Christ's than Satan's—and enjoyed that holy peace which only falls to the share of Christians—, ah, then I could dearly love him who is the cause of all this! And now, in order to obtain forgiveness, I must repent of my sins; & in order to this, I must feel their weight & know their atrocity!

. . .I have grievously sinned once, twice, thrice, within a day, yea, sinned deliberately, tempted the devil instead of being tempted by him. True, for 2 weeks & a half before the present time, . . . I was in prayer frequently, sometimes sincere & heartfelt, but still I sinned even then, when I might have avoided it.

. . .These two weeks & a half . . . are the longest period of comparative righteousness of conduct that I can recollect! Two weeks & a half! & I, a sinner, aged 22 years & more. . . . I turned from sin, not from a detestation of the same, but from a fear of it, for I found that I secretly loved sin! I turned away from sin, from the pit of hell; & looking in an opposite direction, I, of course, beheld the hill of Zion. . . .

But alas! at the end of this time, I sinned again. I suffered a relapse. . . . I did not watch so strictly & so incessantly as I should have done, and fell! . . . Sin, by a desperate effort of obliviousness (inconsideration) became agreeable, & religion lost its hold on me. . . .

Yes! at this moment I was praying; but behold another proof of my weakness! I was praying; & to render my prayer more heartfelt, I rivetted my eyes on the picture of Christ in Gethsemane, when, in the adjoining apartment I heard the sound of music! I forget my desperate case for the moment and listened:

I, however, recovered my attention to myself & wrote this; and I am at this moment the same weak, contemptible, hopeless, & forlorn wretch that I was before that prayer. I again endeavor to expose my heart to the all-seeing eye of the Great Physician & await his time of cure with the determination to hang on his heavenly lips, till I am assured of my restoration. I try to be devoutness itself!

But hark! another favorite strain! & I am as reckless and forgetful as ever of my wickedness & of the Saviour's suffering and death.

Yes, so weak & obstinate is my nature that hardly have I written a sentence on the subject of myself before I forget what I have written. . . . I think of Christ bleeding on the cross & then recollect that he bled for sinners, for me. I ask myself, why did he do all this? I answer, if he had not died, then

At that point the diary breaks off. Presumably Hagen went off to the next chamber to play sinful duets with whoever was producing the diabolical music that had tempted him from prayer. Hagen adds (much later):

It was not until 3 years later that my heart became established in grace, in 1841–42, but I shall never forget that Saturday night in Nazareth Hall, when I struggled in an agony of repentance.

He describes the event more briefly in his autobiography.

Hagen's sins may have been incongruous with the deeply affecting meditations that grew out of his religious desires, but he almost certainly never broke a Commandment, though he might have dented a few experimentally. Pruett, p. 18, gives one example. Hagen liked beer, even though, as a theological student, he was not supposed to have it.

It seems that Hagen and some friends were enjoying some beer in their room one night when they suddenly became aware of the familiar footsteps of their Bishop approaching the door. Evidently the others managed to hide their drinks quickly, and Hagen, not wishing to be caught in a compromising situation, merely took his high silk hat from his head and capped it over his beer on the table. His insistence on formal attire paid off handsomely on that occasion.

Hagen probably laughed about the incident—one can easily imagine his relating it boisterously and entertainingly—but he did suffer genuinely over his high spirits.

Memoir

After a few years, my extremely indiscreet and inconstant ways were partly, but by no means entirely, replaced by somewhat more manliness and intellectual integrity, at least in outward attitude—while as a matter of fact absolutely nothing in my heart had changed. In this lamentable state I arrived in my eighteenth year at Nazareth, in response to a call to enter the school itself as a teacher. In order to put an end to my development of ungodly ways, the Lord sent to me, in the first year of my service, an extremely dangerous sickness that carried me to the brink of the grave, but he allowed me to mend.

The mercy that he showed in not allowing me to die, in spite of my then unredeemed condition, since I should certainly have been lost forever, was so great that I can never thank him enough, not even to all eternity.

The faithfulness with which I was treated during this illness was also an unforgettable occasion of gratitude to God and man. However, hardly was I well that I returned once more to my former sinful ways, and it is said in truth, "And the state of that man was worse than the first." That I am still here, insofar as I am writing this, is a demonstration that God's love and mercy to poor sinful people exceeds all expectations, and that he attached to men's souls so singular a love that he will save them, even as if only snatching a coal from the fire.

The idea that he was a very sinful person served the very useful purpose of rounding out his personality, generating in him a spirit of tolerance that helped him to see that sin can sometimes be funny, as on an occasion that is transmitted by his granddaughter Mary:

> My father told me of one incident. Grandfather was a "circuit rider" among the mountain people for a time. On one of his trips he visited a young couple and their infant child. The couple asked him to baptize their baby & also to marry them. Grandfather of course consented. But he said, "Everything in its proper order,—the marriage ceremony first & then the baptism."

On the other hand, Hagen could be grumpily self-righteous, as for example on 1 August 1886 in Salem, when he records his disgust at

> a dance gotten up by young and old Moravians and young and old Episcopalians, girls and men, and chaperoned by old Moravian and old Episcopalian women, all being representative first class Salem Society people!

He goes on to complain about an earlier party held at the pastor's house—events ended at "near one o'clock in the morning!" Hagen was "grieved" by the frivolity of both events,

> this in the bosom of two of the most pretentious churches in the world, to wit, the Moravian and the Episcopalian of the "modern school". . . . I really thought that Salem was a more Christianlike place than Bethlehem (which is as frivolous as possible), but I mourn over my mistake. The church and town in Bethania equals Salem in refinement and intelligence and far exceeds it in true

Christian life and conduct. . . . May God grant grace to Salem and forgive me if I wrong anyone in my thoughts or in these private memoranda of the day.

Thus Hagen was capable of being naughty when he was a Single Brother and cranky when he was a Widower. I do not hesitate to report his foibles, however, because, although he aimed at perfection, he achieved humanity, which is much more important.

4

Husband, Father, Deacon, Presbyter

Auto-Biography

Very unexpectedly I was sent, after 5 years service in Salem, to Nazareth Hall as [a] teacher. . . .

This assignment lasted from 1837 to 1844, but Hagen made a journey back to Salem in 1841 in order to be married. He was ordained a deacon on 19 September 1844 by William Henry Van Vleck, preached his first sermon at Bethania, North Carolina, 22 September 1844, and was ordained Presbyter by Bishop J. G. Herrmann on 30 November 1851, just before he went to Friedland, North Carolina, as pastor. During this decade Hagen's ministry was as restrained as his unconventional personality allowed it to be, but several experiences clarified his faith and his goals: he underwent a heartfelt conversion that he credited to his wife, he tasted the life of a backwoods preacher, and he stumbled upon early Moravian historical documents, the contents of which were to occupy him for the rest of his life.

It was only after he arrived in York that Hagen began to apply what he had learned between 1841 and 1851, so that it

Francis Florentine Hagen as a young man.

was there that his ministry changed. This chapter summarizes Hagen's life in the decade of the 1840s, completes the chronology of the rest of his life so far as his posts and titles were concerned, and describes the enormously significant documents that came serendipitously into his hands. The chapter following describes what happened to him subsequently to that decade, namely, that he became a Moravian evangelist, a rare ecclesiastical subspecies. Hagen describes, in two slightly different ways, the events that brought on the metamorphosis.

Auto-Biography

On July 1, 1841, I married Sr. Clara Cornelia Reichel, teacher in Salem Female Academy, of which her sainted father, Benjamin F. Reichel, had formerly been principal. My faithful partner's deep piety became the means of leading me to Christ. In a communion service conducted by the late Rev. Charles F. Kluge, then Principal of Nazareth Hall, I saw a ray of light shine into my heart by faith from the Cross of Christ.

I shall remember til to my death [day?] how one Sunday afternoon my heart was so deeply melted at the remembrance how they took the bloody & nailtorn body of Christ from the cross and carried him to Joseph, & how I wished I could have been there & helped to bear him to his grave.

Memoir

After my attachment to sin had reached a certain point, and temporal and eternal damnation stood before my eyes, the desire to live otherwise, with God's gracious guidance, as it were, discovered itself in me: I changed every aspect of my formerly uncommitted life-style, shunned experiments with sin, and undertook to legitimatize myself at least as a moral being.

In 1841 I travelled to Salem and there was married on the 6th of July to the single sister Clara Cornelia Reichel. We betook ourselves back to Nazareth and busied ourselves there with teaching school. During this time I was guided by the Holy Spirit to a spiritual state.

I was often much moved myself and yearned for a conversion of my heart. I prayed often and sought to return to Holy Communion, which I had not attended for a year and a day. I was above all preoccupied with thoughts of how to come to know for sure that I should die in the Lord. And, oh! how graciously the Friend of souls—my soul!—one day touched me in the Holy Communion and imparted to me the blessed assurance, in my heart, that he had died for me. And that certainty has remained with me to this very hour, and I can now say to poor sinners: Now I have found the solid ground to hold my anchor sure. Where else, besides in Jesus' wounds? And there he was, before the world existed, ground unmovingly secure 'till earth and heaven end.

Auto-Biography

I had established, by anguish, a Select School for Young Ladies at Nazareth, but even [then] I had a strong desire to preach Christ & [him] crucified.

The southern P.E.C. requested (26 June 1844) assistance from the northern P.E.C. in the form of an additional minister to serve a complex of churches at Friedberg, Hope, Providence, Bethania, and what was then called the Salem Diaspora.

The matter was put to the Lot, and Hagen was assigned to Bethania. The congregation there, however, objected that Hagen's youth and inexperience would be obstacles to his success in revitalizing that congregation. The P.E.C. sent representatives to convince them otherwise, but the people, having had a succession of young ministers, would not relent. The minutes of 28 July record a letter

from Brn. Reinecke and Jacobsen at Nazareth about Br. Frs. Hagen, who had been designated for Bethania but declined by its committee . . . , report[ing] on the submissive and Christian attitude shown by Br. Hagen when he received this unwelcome news; they pity him much, and assure us that a very favorable change had taken place some time ago in his disposition and conduct and recommend a reconsideration here of his case.

This was done, and Hagen was accepted on a trial basis. The Minutes record (20 September 1844, *R*, p. 5129) that

Br. and Sr. Francis and Clara Hagen had arrived safe and sound from Nazareth with their little daughter, and we shared in their gratitude at their being preserved during a storm on Chesapeake Bay. As had been agreed upon, both were received as acoluths at the Aelt. Confz. on the 18th; the following day, the 19th, Br. Hagen was ordained a deacon of the Moravian Church by Br. Van Vleck in the Gemein Versammlung in the evening.

Hagen had arrived during a drought so severe that the mills could not grind flour, which was therefore in very short supply. On this day, when Hagen reported (27 September 1844, *R*,

p. 4803), the rains came again. "The dear brethren have met us on all sides with great love and kindness." (30 September 1844, *R*, p. 4803): "Today I rode to Pfafftown for the first time on my old black horse that I found here yesterday. I visited 13 families." Hagen was evidently trying to gather a church there, and in Bethania he began to work in his beloved field of music (8 October 1844, *R*, p. 4803): "In the evening we started practice on our church music. The dear people seemed to have great enthusiasm for it." (16 October 1844, *R*, p. 4804): "Held violin instruction for church music."

All was going well, and it was during his stay in Bethania that Hagen began to be more conscious of, and more moved by, early Moravian religious convictions and history than were his brother pastors. What had happened was that he had found the so-called *Blaue Hefte* of spiritual biographies, concerning which he observes in *Landmarks*, p. 23,

> For a long time they were standard textbooks in [Moravian] Theological Seminaries and were found in every parish library throughout the Church. It was in an humble backwoods parsonage in the State of North Carolina that the writer first saw and read these discourses. He forthwith studied them with great ardor. Having experienced in his own soul the truth and power of their teachings, he preached accordingly, and was permitted to witness how wonderfully God confirms this kind of preaching in the conversion of souls. But the writer cannot disguise his sorrow that these old Gospel truths seem impalatable to some modern churchmen, if not entirely strange and unknown.

Hagen, then, viewed the *Blaue Hefte* not as being merely historical documents, but as providing basic truths by which he could live. Furthermore, he had himself experienced in his heart a conversion in exactly the same manner as had the early Moravians. Most of Hagen's colleagues lacked both his historical knowledge and his spiritual experience, and he therefore fell out of step with them. He was closer in spirit to nineteenth-century Methodists, whose convictions resembled those of the eighteenth-century Moravians whom Hagen emulated.

Instead of becoming a Methodist, Hagen became a Moravian evangelist. He began to conduct revivals for his congregations, and he translated the old Moravian documents so that his brethren would understand his historical and spiritual position. Very few ever did.

Hagen lived with these books in and around Salem until 1854, when he moved to York, Pennsylvania. In the next chapter I discuss his work there, which was different from what it had been in the South. However, the present chapter superficially completes the chronicle of Hagen's official appointments and provides extracts from Hagen's own translations of the early documents that brought about his change from a conventional minister to an unconventional evangelist.

Auto-Biography

> From York I was removed to Bethlehem Pa as a member of the Provincial Elders Conference. During this time my faithful and devoted wife died of typhoid fever & now sleeps in the old Bethlehem graveyard.

Clara Cornelia died 30 May 1862, when Hagen was forty-six years old, his children ranging in age from eighteen to only nine. No personal diaries of his are known from that time, so that we know little about what Hagen did during the Civil War. Judging from his reactions to the many troubles that surrounded him in his later years, however, it is likely that he accepted everything as the Lord's will and set about dealing resourcefully with his problems.

On 10 June 1864, a little more than two years after Clara Cornelia had died, Hagen married Ellen Smyser of York, Pennsylvania, and four more children were born during this marriage: William ("Willy") Timoleon, Beatus (stillborn), Ernest Smyser, and Harry Rice. Only the first two children were born in York, for in 1867 Hagen moved to New Dorp, Staten Island, New York.

> After six years at Bethlehem I was sent to New Dorp, Staten Island, N.Y. Three years later I accepted an invitation to labor as City Missionary among the Germans in the City of New York.

In 1869 Hagen went as a delegate to the Synod held in Herrnhut, taking the children with him. In the following year (1 July 1870), he began ministering to the many Germans on Manhattan Island, preaching in Olivet Chapel and in Calvary Chapel on Spring Street, making house calls, and delivering tracts. He was unbelievably busy. During August, September, and October 1870, for example, Hagen gave out 2,000 tracts to people in the street, delivered 30 sermons, conducted 36 prayer meetings, made 400 calls at people's homes, and collected $70.00 in offerings, to which the Church added $97.00 by way of supporting him. It was always like that. On New Year's Eve 1870, he wrote,

Ellen Smyser Hagen.

It is true I carry many cares out of the old into the new year, but have cast them on the Lord who careth for us. . . . When one feels the pinchings of poverty at home, one can all the better sympathize with others who are in the same boat!

He had greater troubles ahead of him, however.

After three years service there, my wife (Ellen W. Smyser of York) died suddenly of cerebral spinal miningitis [*sic*], & now sleeps in New Dorp Cemetery. This crushing blow so greatly hindered my work as city missionary that I applied to the governing board at Bethlehem for a smaller charge. I was accordingly sent to Iowa & took charge of Harmony, Victor, & North Salem in Poweshick C°.

Ellen died on 2 April 1872, after only eight years of marriage. Hagen again found himself, this time at age fifty-seven, with the care of young children: three boys, aged seven, four, and

Ernest Smyser Hagen.

two. There was probably no one to help him, since even the youngest child of his first marriage (Felix, then aged nearly seventeen) would in those days have been independent or about to become so.

The troubles that piled up during Hagen's later years would have overwhelmed a lesser man: his health deteriorated, and a forced retirement caused straitened financial circumstances and difficult domestic arrangements. Throughout that trying time, however, Hagen focused his determination, his faith, and his every physical, mental, and spiritual power on two cardinal tasks: to provide for his three youngest children and to preserve through evangelism the integrity of the doctrine of the Redemption. Those two tasks were to converge in Ernest, because he was the only one of Hagen's seven sons who was to become a minister and evangelist; but Hagen was close also to both Willie and Harry.

While he was in the Midwest Hagen learned that he had been put on the retired list. His reaction to the news was bitter and emotional, but he eventually accustomed himself to his new status. He became a part-time or temporary pastor in various Pennsylvania towns and made the memorable farewell visit to his boyhood home described in Chapter 2. He then took up quarters with his son Ernest, first in York, and finally in Lititz, where he died.

From his arrival in York in 1854 until his final temporary pastorate in Easton, Pennsylvania, in 1888, Hagen had devoted his life and works to the models and philosophies set forth in the *Blaue Hefte* and in other documents that he collected, translated, and used, such as sermons and discourses by Zinzendorf; a manuscript, *Grosser Conferenz Syllabus*, which belonged at one time to Peter Böhler; and some early material that had been handed down in the family. For example, on 31 December 1886, one of his aunts, Mrs. Kraemer in Salem, gave him

> several autograph letters of Bishop Spangenberg and . . . the MS memoirs of his departed wife . . . ; an MS address by Christian Gregor; and . . . 2 memoirs (a funeral address by old Br. C. G. Reichel) . . . and a sermon by William Cooper . . . published at Herrnhut Feb. 13, 1799.

Hagen's complete eight-volume handwritten translation of the Böhler manuscript was never published and is still to be found in the northern Moravian archives, but he did bring out two works that were based upon it. The first was his "Pia desideria," a set of historical studies that he published in fifteen installments in the first volume of the *Moravian*, one every three or four weeks from January to December 1856. The second was the book *Old landmarks, or faith and practice of the Old Moravian Church at the time of its revival and restoration in 1727 and twenty years after*, which he published in 1886. "Desideria" is short and polemical; it has been completely forgotten. *Landmarks* is longer and historical; many Moravians know about it, but few have actually read it.

Although the Moravian Church is probably the oldest Protestant denomination, it has always been one of the smallest (there are only two hundred thousand Moravians in the world today, fifty thousand of them in the Americas). Therefore, practically every writer about a Moravian subject feels compelled to explain who the Moravians are, so that dreary little historical prefaces become almost standard in published books.

Hagen noticed this tendency even in his day, and in "Pia desideria" no. 4, he asks, "Why do our church essayists forever dish up Moravian history?" His answer to the question, however, is spiritual, as was typical of him, rather than explanatory, as was typical of everybody else. His goal was to get Moravians to respond to the Word as did their forefathers.

> In that happy time, the Moravian people were not conscious of having any preference for any particular protestant denomination; their thoughts and conversation were only of Jesus and of his power to save. . . . This was the ground of their profession, and this they boldly proclaimed, fearing no cross, no shame, neither persecution nor even death itself.

In no. 8 Hagen lays out chronologically the early metamorphoses of Moravian theology:

> . . . 1722–1727, Christ given for us. . . . 1727–1734, Christ living in us, and the full assurance of faith. . . . 1734–1743, "Christ given for us" as being the foundation of instantaneous justification and sanctification. . . . 1743–1754, "Blood-theology" and other hyper-evangelical errors. . . . 1754–1760, return to the teachings of 1727–1734.

In no. 12 he describes

> a species of Quietism [that] stole over the Moravian Church . . . as early as the year 1739. . . . From this time we date the past and present imbecility of Moravianism.

In no. 13 he urges much more extensive and frequent meetings in small groups for prayer and conversation.

> A spirit of religious inquiry will be aroused, persons will meet together for mutual edification, conversations will multiply, and the church be revived.

In the final no. 15, Hagen concludes by recording

> his firm conviction that we must return to the doctrine and practice of the church as it was in the year 1727 and during the subsequent decade,

and in *Landmarks*, p. 28, he summarizes his goal:

> The distinctive and fundamental idea of the original Moravian Brethren was that it is possible to establish on earth a true, visible, palpable Church of Jesus Christ. . . .

Hagen understood early Moravianism so well that it is almost as if he had experienced, rather than merely studied, the events. Therefore, instead of attempting in my own words to describe the matrix that created this remarkable man, I shall let him do so in selections from his own translation of the Böhler manuscript, as he relayed it in *Landmarks*. The story begins with Zinzendorf's narrative, p. 63, of the Commencement of Herrnhut. The refugees had established themselves on the Count's estate.

> The Rev. Mr. Schwedler, a man of great power and unction, once spent a Sunday, . . . the 2^d of July 1727, [in the settlement]. The Count preached in Herrnhut, the Rev. Mr. Rothe in the graveyard, and Pastor Schwedler in Berthelsdorf . . . , one mile north of Herrnhut. . . . All three places were thronged with hearers. A preaching-stand having been put up in the open air, the Word of God was preached to a great multitude. It was *then* that the breath of the Lord came upon them, and a great work of grace commenced, which continued, without interruption, throughout the remainder of the year. In Herrnhut the work became very powerful. Meetings for praise, prayer, and religious conference followed each other in quick succession.

Hagen then continues with his translation of an account by Spangenberg, p. 64.

> A remarkable work of grace commenced under the preaching of several brethren. On the 9th of July there was an unusual excitement in Herrnhut. On this day bands and class-meetings were established. Concerning these meetings Zinzendorf subsequently declared that "without them the Brethren's Church would never have become what it was."

The reference is to the Moravian communal system, with its groupings of people into "choirs" [Hagen's "bands"] by age, sex, and marital status. The account then describes briefly the events of the next several days, all of them filled with meetings of increasing intensity. Finally,

> The Holy Supper was celebrated at Berthelsdorf, and all hearts were melted in love.

Other significant days followed, and Hagen summarizes, on p. 66, as follows:

> The great revival at Herrnhut in July and August 1727 gave the first impulse to subsequent Moravian life and activity, which fact

is to this day annually commemorated by the great Moravian Festival of the Thirteenth of August.

Hagen saw no reason why these events should not take place again, just as they had in the past. All that was required was inward personal conversion. Indeed, accounts of his own revivals read very similarly. He writes on p. 59,

> They partake of the spirit of Paul, Luther, Zinzendorf, Peter Böhler, John Wesley, George Whitefield, etc. . . .

Hagen next describes, on p. 67, the development of systems of personal visitation and

> religious conferences, or as they are now called, experience or testimony meetings, in one place, for singing, speaking, and prayer. . . . But these meetings gradually gave way to liturgies in prose and poetry, of a recitative, antiphonal, and choral character. They were meant to be substitutes for improvised prayer. . . . It is to be feared that in many cases these forms are, as it were, mere grave-clothes wherewith dead souls are bound about. . . , the cold shroud of formalism.

That is to say, the Renewed Moravian Church had begun to change even in Zinzendorf's time. Hagen sought, as he writes on p. 68, a literal modern return to the time of the first renewal.

> Long after liturgical forms had been introduced, Zinzendorf and Christian David declared that free prayer and open testimony are natural and necessary elements in the commencement and proper conduct of great revivals. [Hagen at this point cites Croeger's *Letters of Christian David*.] And it has been so ever since the day of Pentecost. . . . [Hagen, p. 74, quotes Zinzendorf.] Moravianism does not consist of outward forms.

Nevertheless, Hagen admits, on p. 45, that

> . . . every man who calls himself a Christian must have a creed. . . . The different articles of the Moravian faith are contained in the hymnals and catechisms of that church. . . .

Hagen exempted from that generalization the Bethlehem hymnal of 1876, without explaining why.

All other matters were secondary, though important, and Hagen treats them one by one. He translates a particularly powerful passage from the *Extract of the Constitution* of 1733:

> In all things which do not immediately concern the spiritual king-

dom of Christ, we simply, and without contradicting, obey the
higher powers. But with regard to conscience, the liberty of this
one cannot suffer to be in any way limited or abridged. . . . We
. . . are determined, God being our helper, to give up not only
our goods (as we did before) but life itself, rather than this liberty
which God hath given us.

Hagen describes, on p. 103, the peculiar "diaspora" of the
Moravian Church, whereby, according to Clemens, the Moravian *jura* (translated by Hagen as "church-order") existed
"within the pale of . . . the Lutheran Church" or, on p. 107, the
Reformed, as required by the State. Moravians avoided prose-
lyting, because their allegiance was to an inward and spiritual
phenomenon.

They nevertheless showed due respect to other Churches. . . .
They carefully abstained from disparaging [them]. . . . (p. 55)
They gladly adopted whatever modes and measures of other
churches they found more efficient than their own.

Hagen makes the point, on p. 77, that Moravian governance
is presbyterial, so that bishops were needed only for the rite of
ordination and were, even in that regard, dispensable:

Apostolicity consists in having the spirit of the Apostles and not
in mere Episcopal succession.

Hagen explains this point and its ramifications for the Moravian Church in an article "The Thirteenth of November," which
was probably published in the *Moravian*, and which he pasted
into his scrapbook.

This memorial day of the Moravian Church dates from a Conference held at London, on Lamb's Conduit Place, Red Lion Street,
in the year 1741. The conference commenced on the 11th of September and ended on the 23d.

Referring to an extract of the minutes of that conference,
Hagen lists the conclusions. The ministers reported on their
departments, and the bishops on the general state of the
church. Leonhard Dober was functioning as President, and he
was to report on the whole work of the Church. The significant
statement was made that

when the Saviour is in our midst, we must embrace the opportunity and open our souls to all the gracious influences which he
sheds around. . . .

Hagen observes that

> at this conference a modification of the government of the Church was resolved upon. It was attended by a remarkable occasion of faith, love, and devotion to Christ as the Head of the Church, and made in the year 1741, a memorial year of the church.
>
> At a subsequent Synod held at Hirschberg, July 1743, it was resolved (in the XXI Session, July 10th, p.m.) that the Elders' Festival (Aeltesten Fest) of the ministers should be celebrated on the 16th of September, and that the churches (Orts Gemeinen) on the 13th of November.

Hagen then turns to an account by Louis de Schrautenbach, a contemporary of Zinzendorf's, to tell what happened.

> The churches had increased in number, and each one had its own elders. One man was General Elder and had the care of all the churches. All new projects, and every thing of importance, were laid before him, as the leading man in every Conference, whose opinion and decision was always accepted as final. John Leonhard Dober, the founder of the mission in St. Thomas, the first and foremost of that devoted band of Gospel-heroes who were at that time going through the heathen world, a venerable, wise, and devoted man, bore this office.
>
> Zinzendorf being on the point of leaving for America, Leonhard felt that the burden of this office would be too heavy for him to bear alone. . . . He resigned the office.
>
> At this Conference, a successor was to have been appointed; but the brethren soon found that there was no one in whom all the qualifications, which had made Leonhard's administration so successful, were combined. At last one of the brethren proposed to dispense with the office of General Elder, and to confide all the more in the government of the Great Head of the Church, even Jesus Christ.
>
> This idea found instant favor with all the brethren; . . . there was great emotion throughout the entire Church, accompanied by new vows of allegiance to Christ. . . .

The work of the former Chief Elder was distributed among several brethren who were designated Vice Elders, and thus came into existence the ecclesiastical hierarchy peculiar to the Moravian Church, in which Christ is the literal Head.

This fact led to another characteristic tradition, now unfortunately set aside, namely, the Lot, which Hagen describes on p. 99 of *Landmarks*. He explains that it was used in the belief that

the Head and Chief Shepherd of the Church would condescend
to reveal his will . . . by this means when all other means—
human, scriptural, or providential—failed to give . . . light.

Hagen then turns, on p. 113, to missions, summarizing their
history and calling them the *pièce de résistance* of the Moravian
Church. The end of the book, Part III, p. 116ff., is devoted to
"Original papers illustrative of the faith and practice of the
Brethren." He transmits much material by Wesley and numerous official statements that emanated from the settlement of
Herrnhaag, which the Moravians abandoned in 1750 on account of a clash with the State. He also translates the diaries of
several missionaries. He concludes, p. 233,

> Each individual and each generation must begin religious life
> in the same way and at the same point, and that point is a
> personal and experimental knowledge of salvation by the revi-
> sion of sins. This momentous experience can alone lift men, indi-
> vidually and collectively, to the same plane of vital Christianity.

Everything that Hagen did was controlled from these basic
beliefs. Every aspect of his complicated character and all the
products of his varied talents must be understood within the
context of his love of, and commitment to, Jesus his Saviour.

Having thus arrived at a firm religious faith through at least
two metaphysical experiences, Hagen became insatiably curious about all kinds of religious manifestations and involved
himself with a great many different groups of believers. On 16
March 1846 (*R*, p. 5160), for example, he asked and received
permission "to attend a public union meeting of various ministers near Bethania," without saying that all the other ministers
were Methodists.

He also visited other groups purely as a religious observer, a
kind of theological tourist. On 27 September 1870 (diary), for
example, he

> dropped into a Jewish synagogue and witnessed their New
> Year's festivities which are in progress. Old Jews in old white
> headdresses, old white surplices, dingy-looking white and yel-
> low shawls; and young Jews in smart clothes, with fine new silk
> hats on their heads, and with here and there a broad white silk
> scarf thrown over their shoulders, went in and out of the church
> ad libitum & worshipped, hats on the head, out of Hebrew pray-
> erbooks. The officiating minister sang the prayer in Italian opera
> style with marvellous modulation of voice but very musically (&
> artistically so), the congregation chiming in occasionally. In the
> interval between his operatic warbles the people read aloud, but

also in musical tones & cadences. Meanwhile conversations are going on among the people & the utmost freedom of ingress & egress is allowed, but still a great deal of order & decorum is maintained. The singing in the Rivington Synagogue was delightful.

On 5 October 1879, he again

went into the Jewish Temple on 5th Avenue & witnessed their rites on their great Atonement Day. I also heard a sermon on the "moral power" which the Jews inherit from their fathers. . . .

While in Blairstown, Iowa, Hagen (29 April 1878)

went to the Colony of Inspired Ones, commonly called Amana Colony. They emigrated from Wetteravia, near Frankfurt, Germany. Met some who were formerly members of our church at Neuwied, and others from Marienborn, Herrnhaag, and Ronneburg. The people at Amana are well aware of Zinzendorf's relation with Dr. Fr. Rock, which had not been altogether of a very friendly nature, but I was met with much cordiality.

The colony consists of churches governed by elders and located on a tract of land numbering about 30,000 acres, population about 2000. It is in a very flourishing condition; stores, factories, mills, and farms are excellent, and their mode of life very Christian-like, plain but comfortable, and as far as eating and drinking are concerned, almost luxurious. They dress plain, eat 5 times a day, and work leisurely but well. This Colony is a model of excellent agriculture, gardening, vine culture, and superior manufactures.

All are German. Their towns resemble, and are even more quiet and better ordered than, our best Moravian towns, so far as my observation went. They dress uniformly and have their meals in common. Each congregation has from 12 to 14 dining houses. No beer nor wine or intoxicating drinks are sold, but to friends visiting them, beer and wine of the best quality are offered with unstinted hospitality, but all this within the bounds of the strictest sobriety. Americans are utterly confounded, when they see how well the German knows to keep asunder the use and abuse of the above named good cheer—and after seeing this, got new ideas on the subject!

I procured their catechism and find them perfectly sound on the Doctrine of the Atonement and in their faith in the Divinity of Christ.

They differ with us merely 1. in setting aside infant Baptism; 2. in their belief in a millenial fire of purification after death, for those who do not die regenerate (Reinigungsfeuer) &c.; 3. in another purification after their millenium [sic] for those who are rejected in the Judgment Day, the Lake of Fire (Zorufeuer) [?];

4. in the final restitution of all things and the eventual salvation
of all mankind after many "ages" or "eternities" of purifying
torment in God's wrath and fire. But all men will finally be saved,
tho' as by fire! 5. They also believe in special inspirations,
through a voice from heaven, heard by the spiritually minded
Christian.

They are, however, very exclusive and admit no one to their
private church assemblies and do not give any publicity to their
doctrine and constitution and are far removed from proselytism
or from any species of mission work, except that of selling excellent goods of their own manufacture at fair prices.

Hagen seems to have visited as many denominations as he
could. On 14 January 1886, for example, he "spoke 3 p.m. in
Salvation Army barracks," and while living in Tremont (25 August 1882) he "attended Colored campmeeting above High
Bridge at 3 p.m., and during one prayer meeting after the sermon I spoke a few words." Nearly forty years before (R,
p. 5145, 9 May 1845) Hagen had solicited permission to organ-
ize . . . the negroes at Bethania and vicinity . . . as a small
society and continue to administer baptism and communion
with them." The conference had no objection, but urged Hagen
to "make detailed inquiry from the Bethania committee regard-
ing this."

Hagen also visited liturgical churches. He involved himself
in Episcopalian Parochial Missions on the 19th, 21st, and 22nd
of March 1879, which, he said (19 March 1879), "resemble protracted meetings and are held likewise by the Roman Catholics." Hagen also occasionally attended regular services at the
Episcopal Church, as he did, for example, on 29 October 1879
in Bethlehem. Not everything the Episcopalians did pleased
him, but, interestingly, he was less comfortable with the Lutherans, even though Zinzendorf's Lutheran connection had
created an early affinity between the Lutherans and the Moravians. On Friday, 8 March 1878, for example, he

> Read burial service at the grave of Hans Peter Hansen, aged
> about 18. Died of typhoid fever at the house of Mr. Black. . . . He
> is the only one of the family in the country. Three more of Mr.
> Black's family are sick, the oldest son very dangerously. The
> funeral sermon was postponed, and only the burial services were
> held at the grave, partly in order that the other sick ones in the
> house might not hear of the death of poor Hansen, and also in
> order to afford all their Lutheran friends an opportunity of being
> present at the funeral, for the deceased was a Lutheran, and
> Lutheran services are deemed indispensable.

There is no denomination so rigidly exclusive in these parts, the Catholics excepted, as the Old Lutherans: my services were called in only on account of the unfortunate absence of Rev. Baird, Lutheran, who, I presume, is the one who will preach the postponed funeral sermon. Proficiat! But is it not the same with all denominations, our own not excepted?

Hagen was somewhat closer to the Albright Methodists. This denomination was formally organized in about 1816 in New Berlin, Pennsylvania, as the Evangelical Association (now part of the Methodist Church), by followers of Jacob Albright (1759–1808). In Blairstown, 2 December 1877, he observed that

We will get few Lutherans and Reformed unless they are connected among us. German Methodists (Albrights) who abound here, are, in the language of the German Reformed preacher, Rev. Feige in Marengo, "spoiled" for any other church, i.e., Reformed or Lutheran, but they are not spoiled, I trust, for the Kingdom of heaven nor for the Moravian Church, as long as the latter is true to itself and does not forget its holy calling, which is to be a Church of Jesus Christ.

Indeed, the first Moravian services were held in the Blairstown Albright church, rented for $1.50 per service; and while visiting in Hazleton, Pennsylvania, (21 September 1879) Hagen preached "in the evening in the Albright Church, to many hearers."

There are other examples of his involvement with the "German Methodists," but Hagen appears to have been especially attracted to English Methodism, often preaching in the Bethlehem Methodist churches (16 March and 21 September 1870, for example). On 25 July 1886, he records that he

attended the fine M. E. Church in Winston and heard the Rev. Scroggs. This is one of the most beautiful and tasteful churches I have ever seen, far more chaste and proper in character than the Salem church, which is very gay above and grave below, the upper part being gaudy stencil-work, and the lower dark umber walnut color, and taken all in all, of the bucolic type! The preaching in the two churches corresponds with their respective architectural tastes.

On Sunday, 23 August 1886, Hagen preached at a Methodist revival to which he had been taken by one of the Hausers, some of whom were Moravians-turned-Methodists. Hagen was very gratified by the event, which had a large attendance, including some Bethania Moravians such as "Uncle Joseph

Transou." The next day, upon his return to Salem, Hagen was quite ill, and observed, "There's but a step between me and death, and therefore I must keep quiet. Yet it is hard to refuse to preach when asked. Br. Hunt has other help, and the fact is that I was present at the invitation of his Methodist membership."

During his stay in Tremont (August and September 1882), Hagen attended the Methodist Church there very regularly—so frequently, that he seemed to be almost a member—; and when his son Ben, after a long absence from any church, finally joined that same congregation in Tremont, Hagen was, as we have seen, overjoyed. His main concern, in keeping with Moravian custom, was not denominationalism, but Jesus Christ and his redeeming blood.

5
Evangelist

Zinzendorf was two centuries ahead of his time and therefore offended a great many people; Hagen was only a century ahead of his time, but he managed to offend nearly as many. On 31 August 1886, Salem was rocked by a geological earthquake, and during the following three months, Salem experienced theological aftershocks that are described later in this chapter. God was, of course, responsible for both events, but Hagen had more than a little to do with the latter. He spent forty years in preparing for the event, which was, in view of his theological outlook and North Carolina's geological status, inevitable.

It is a tendency of all religions to begin with revolutionary fervor; once established, they fall into habitual conservatism, deriving nourishment not from new and exciting ideas but from old and traditional procedures. Both stages are effective, because there are always some people who like ferment and others who like placidity.

When Hagen was a boy, Salem was a closed Moravian community that was still in the last part of its revolutionary period. When he returned to Salem as an old man, it had already been thirty years since it had been opened up to non-Moravians, and it had passed over into a new period of adjustment to conservative mainstream American religion. Hagen loved Salem but

Francis Florentine Hagen and William Henry Rice. A possible time when this picture might have been taken is the beginning of Rice's pastorate in York, i.e., 1868. Another picture of Rice appears in Albright opposite p. 176.

found its religious life exasperatingly superficial; Salem loved him but regarded his earthy revivalism with bewilderment. He was aware of the strife he was causing, but since he had spent the last twenty-five years of his life expecting to die, he found that it saved time, of which he thought that he had little left, to be reverberant rather than diplomatic. John F. Hagen observes about him,

> He had a vivid personality and rarely did a smile leave his face. His hearty laugh saved many a strained situation. His conversation was sparkling though somewhat explosive. His sentences frequently ended in a loud crescendo which often startled the stranger. He felt what he said and never permitted a conversation to end in bitterness.

Auto-Biography

> When the writer saw the light of this world, my father dedicated him to the gospel ministry, saying "that he should finish what he was unable to when crippled in the Indian Mission in America."

John F. Hagen continues ("Memories"),

> Grandfather was a preacher of power. According to my late father, Rev. Ernest S. Hagen, D.D., his preaching was a fine example of the "truth using the man instead of man using the truth."

Hagen improvised almost all of his sermons, but two were written out. One was the memorial sermon on the death of Senseman (see Appendix 4), and the other was the first sermon he ever delivered (22 September 1844) in his first pastorate at Bethania, North Carolina. He made it the subject of some *Rhymes* that he wrote on his eighty-first birthday in 1896:

> Grace for grace I've since obtained,
> Greatest grace of all I gained,
> When I had "A Call" to thunder
> Forth the Truth—O mighty wonder!—
>
> . . . .
>
> In that gracious year of yore,
> Eighteenth hundred forty-four,
> My poor lips began to stammer,
> Whilst the Lord, with gospel hammer
>
> Broke the stony hearts of men,
> Righteous and great sinners, when
> Mourning, weeping, they salvation
> Found in Jesus Christ's oblation.

The manuscript of that first sermon is in the Foundation collections, donated in 1983 by Elizabeth Hagen Pfaff. If frequency of sermonizing is any indication of merit, Hagen must have been capable, because it would be a difficult task merely to list the dates when he held forth in his old age. Furthermore, he preached in an enormous number of different Moravian churches and in many churches of other denominations. On a trip to Salem, 17 September–1 November 1885, for example, Hagen preached at Friedberg, Salem, Bethania, and Kernersville; between 11 April and 13 June 1886, he preached at Bethania, Olivet, Bethabara, Friedland, East Salem, Wachovia Arbor, Mt. Tabor, and New Philadelphia, sometimes more than once, and often in spite of poor health or bad weather—and always traveling either behind a horse or on foot.

In addition to the Bible, one of his main sources for his sermons must have been the sermons of Zinzendorf. Hagen owned and studied them, and he completed at York his translation of *Zinzendorf's Pennsylvania Sermons* and issued a large and handsome prospectus, a copy of which is in the MMF collections, soliciting advance subscribers at $1.25 a copy, which was to contain "about 400 pages, printed in large clear type on good book paper neatly and strongly bound in cloth and sent post free." Hagen describes the contents as follows:

> Count Zinzendorf, the distinguished Moravian clergyman, landed at New York, Dec. 2, 1741, and a few days later reached Philadelphia, which city he had at first designed to make the centre of his activity during his sojourn in Pennsylvania. With the exception of three months spent among the Indians, he itinerated in the rural districts east of the Susquehanna, filled the pulpits of Reformed and Lutheran congregations which were unsupplied with pastors, conducted religious convocations, wrote numerous papers and esays—some theological, others controversial and apologetical—, and carried on a large correspondence. In January of 1743 he returned to Europe.
>
> . . . The Count's sermons were extemporaneous, but remarkably systematic, logical, scriptural, teeming with illustrations, striking epigrams, and a surprising amount of historical information, and well worthy of a liberal effort to publish them. The translator is happy to contribute his mite to this end, in presenting his manuscript to the publication fund, as a free gift, and a labor of love which has already had its own reward, in the happiness which it has afforded him.

The labor was all the reward Hagen was to receive, because the manuscript was never published and is now in the Archives of the Northern Province. It is an excellent piece of

work, and could well be published in our day as a memorial
both to Zinzendorf and to Hagen.

The prospectus lists the twenty-seven sermons, giving the
exact scriptural basis, the date, place, title, and sometimes even
the hour of delivery. A few of the sermons immediately preceded or followed the count's American journey.

One wonders why the manuscript was never published. A
possible reason may lie in Hagen's evident inability to resist
controversy. He says, in connection with the last sermon, delivered by Zinzendorf

> in the newly erected Moravian Church in Philadelphia at 7:30 in
> the evening immediately before his final departure from Pennsyl-
> vania. In his closing prayer the Count invoked God's blessing on
> all who had opposed him in his labours, such as Henry Antes,
> the family of John Stepen Benezet, the Lutheran Church war-
> dens, and Brother John Bechtel in Germantown.
>
> These, together with many others whose names could not be
> publicly mentioned, were either members or ministers of the
> Lutheran, Reformed, Baptist, and Quaker churches and zealous
> supporters of the cause of Christ. His prayer for those who had
> opposed him are exceedingly touched and Christ-like. And thus
> he parted from Pennsylvania, with brotherly love, and universal
> charity.

Hagen's statements are really quite innocent: to him the controversy was all in the past, but it is easy to imagine how this
description must have irritated almost the entire prospective
readership.

Nor were the Pennsylvania sermons Hagen's only Zinzendorf translations, for the diary entry for 22 July 1886 tells us "I
am engaged in translating Zinzendorf's *Berlin Discourses* and
finished the 1st on Sat. 24." 4 August 1886: "Translation ad-
vanced to p. 58 MSS"; 24 August 1886; "Am quite busy this
week in translating the *Berlin Discourses*, a work which grows in
interest and profitableness to my soul, as I progress with it";
and 30 November 1886:

> Completed my translation of Zinzendorf's 16 Discourses on
> Luther's Explanation of the Second Article of the Augsburg Con-
> fession, held in Berlin in the year 1738. Whatever difficulty at-
> tended this undertaking, it was amply compensated by the spiri-
> tual profit and pleasure derived from it by the translation. A
> Translator's preface and a translation of the Author's preface,
> and the Editor's [Gottfried Clemens] Postscript, yet remain to be
> completed. I commenced this translation July 5th of the present

year and spent exactly 5 months in finishing the work, i.e., July 5 to Nov. 30, '86.

Five years after my religious experience, I received a call as Pastor of the Church at Bethany (Bethania) in North Carolina. While there I read Count Zinzendorf's sermons, which strengthened & deepened my love for my Redeemer. During the first year of my ministry here, 1844–1845, I had the happiness of participating in a great revival of religion at a "union meeting" under the united efforts of 4 local Methodist preachers & myself. Many were converted during this blessed season. A similar great revival had taken place at Friedland, Br. Lewis Rights being pastor, which even so surprised the Quakers, who had a settlement nearby, that they exclaimed, "The Holy Ghost has been poured out upon the Dutch/Germans."

The Quakers were not alone in being surprised; so were the Moravians, and their surprise was to turn to consternation. Hagen, however, was just getting started down a path that he was to follow the rest of his life, namely, that of the evangelist. He began to be involved to a certain degree in circuit riding, especially in the mountains on the border of Virginia and North Carolina. The Conferenz reported (R, p. 5197, 26 October 1847) receiving

> the latest report submitted by the Brn. Hagen and Zevely regarding their visits in the mountains of Virginia, as to the petition signed by 30 persons for a minister and teacher of their own at Volunteer Gap, for which 300 acres of land are available at $102.

Auto-Biography

A new life infused into the Southern Province through these remarkable revivals, and two new churches were formed: Mt. Bethel Blue Ridge Mission and Macedonia, beyond the Yadkin River, 1855. To this day protracted meetings are held in the South, and many new churches have been formed.

Brn. Bahnson and L. Reichel described the dedication of a new building at Macedonia in the *Moravian*, 1/24, 13 June 1856, p. 186, as follows.

> "Come over and help us!" has been for some time past the Macedonian cry, resounding from beyond the river which separates Davie from Forsyth county. Br. Hagen, at that time minister at Friedberg, not only heard but cheerfully responded to this call,

and commenced preaching in a school-house in the woods. Br.
Rights continued the work with the evident blessing of the Lord.
The nucleus of a congregation having been collected, this mere
handful of disciples undertook the erection of a log meeting-
house, which . . . was finished this spring.

The 24th and 25th of May were set apart for the solemn dedication of this house of the Lord, and several of the ministering
brethren at Salem, accompanied by part of the musical staff,
prepared to "praise the Lord with the sound of the trumpet," . . .
went over to "help" in the solemn services of the day.

The weather being fine, and the interest and sympathy of the
surrounding country having been awakened, so great a con-
course of people had assembled in the forest shade, that hardly
the third part could have been crowded together in the newly
erected house. Therefore the solemn dedicatory services . . .
were conducted . . . in God's own temple of nature, under the
stately oaks of the forest.

Bishop Jacobson opened the services with a few introductory
remarks . . . and in virtue of his office, pronounced the solemn
dedication prayer. . . . Br. Bahnson presented a large quarto Bible
to the congregation on behalf of the Salem Bible Association, and
Br. Reichel closed the services by communicating a letter addressed by Br. Hagen to the members and friends of this new
church.

After an interval of about one hour, in which by an interchange
of hospitalities the wants of the outer man were amply supplied,
the sweet sounds of our solemn church tunes called the assembly
together, when Br. Reichel preached on Ps. xxvi. 8, Br. Bahnson
closing with prayer.

A desire was manifested by the people to have a meeting after
sundown. Hence some of the members of the Friedberg congregation, having found a lodging-place nearer by, . . . conducted
the meeting, which according to their testimony proved both
pleasant and profitable.

The next day being the Lord's own day, the people wended
their way to the consecrated spot at an early hour, and in large
numbers, approaching from every direction, although scarcely
visible on account of the density of the forest, until they had
reached the immediate neighbourhood of the preachers' stand.
They might have been seen hastening on, some in showy carriages, others in plain farm wagons, some on horseback, others
on foot.

Not least conspicuous among the large crowd were the col-
oured people, many of them on horseback, and all decked out in
their Sunday best, not unfrequently exhibiting quite a stately
appearance; the females sporting spotless white or silken
dresses, veils, and bonnets, of the most approved fashion. The
benches provided for the purpose, not being able to accommo-
date all present, some remained seated in their carriages, or

brought to the spot the chairs on which they had sat in their wagons. . . . Close by the stand, the carriage containing the musicians occupied a conspicuous position, and the sweet and solemn strains sent forth by these brethren, made it an object observed by all. . . , while farther in the background were seen two large stages, which, together with numerous other vehicles, had brought to the spot a large representation of the Salem congregation.

The spot on which we met is one of interesting associations. During the period which tried men's souls, when stout men and patriotic women by the help of a just and merciful God, secured to their country that liberty which their descendants still enjoy, strains of martial music could have been heard, at no very great distance, as the leader of the hostile army crossed the river, and soon after engaged in battle with the patriots opposing his progress. Today, for the first time on the Lord's day, music was there heard again, but it was solemn, and sent forth an invitation to the scattered multitude to assemble beneath the venerable giants of the forest, there to raise their hearts in sincere gratitude and adoration, from nature to nature's God, and the Author of eternal salvation.

About 11 o'clock, the soul-stirring sound of the trombones called together around the stand of the preachers, as many as had ears to hear; and Br. Bahnson spoke. . . . Towards the close of the service, which had been preceded by a collection in aid of the new house of prayer, the sky became overcast, and very soon the mutterings of an approaching thunder storm began. . . . A large number . . . fled in great haste. . . . But . . . those who ventured to remain had scarcely any rain. . . .

After those who remained on the spot had partaken of a hasty dinner, served up in primitive style, the trombones again sounded with sweet Moravian tunes, inviting all who were still present to come and listen once more to the glad tidings of salvation. . . . Br. Rights preached on Luke vi. 19. . . . With fervent prayer and supplication that the Lord would be graciously pleased not to let his word return unto him void, . . . Br. Rights closed this interesting meeting; and all who love the Lord and his blood-bought church, will unite in supplicating the Saviour to visit our Macedonia with his salvation, and to make that lonely forest house of prayer the happy spot where many may find Christ precious to their immortal souls. . . .

Hagen had brought this church into existence, and it was inevitable that he should become an evangelist. His father had been a German blacksmith who had been moved to become a missionary. Hagen had been born, raised, and educated in the two closed religious communities of Salem and Nazareth. Two religious experiences of almost Augustinian intensity had placed Jesus first in his life. He had persistently explored other religious manifestations. He could not understand why the Moravians were so cold, in view of their historical involvement in intense spiritual experiences.

Auto-Biography

I will not enlarge on the topic of religious excitements, but simply point to Gethsemane, where the Author of Salvation prayed & agonized with strong cries and tears, & to Golgotha & to Pentecost & to some scenes in Herrnhut in the year 1727. Outside of our circle one sees the same among Methodists, Baptists, Presbyterians & other churches who have any vitality.

It would appear that Hagen's first revivals occurred early in his pastorate in York, Pennsylvania.

Auto-Biography

In 1855 I was called to York, Pa, as successor to Pastor Ambrose Rondthaler. At York it pleased the Lord to favor our church with a powerful revival in 1857, which extended into the country at Naumans' [?] School House, Weigelstown [?] west of York and Conway's [?] School House south of York, where many souls were brought in [?].

Hagen began to visit other congregations. He mentions in his diary on 28 October 1855 that in a lovefeast being held in Fifth Moravian Church, Philadelphia, he "expressed a loving wish that God might help that Church with a revival. Br. Baker & Blum immediately took it up." The next several entries in his diary record its evidently successful course.

Hagen visited Gnadenhutten, Ohio, between 13 and 21 March 1857 and conducted what appears from his diary to have been a revival there. He preached once or twice a day and also traveled (18 March 1857) to Fry's Valley to preach. The Dover, Ohio, diary reports that Hagen returned to Fry's Valley on 14 November 1857 to dedicate a new church, and then continued to Gnadenhutten, where he remained until 17 November 1857, preaching there once or twice a day. (Lawrence Hartzel kindly searched these diaries.)

Hagen's work at York was evangelical. Albright on, p. 168, tells us that there was a general revivalistic trend in the country at that time that furthered a new type of evangelism foreign to the quiet manners of the brethren, with the result that when Rev. Hagen adopted these unusual methods of approach, many of the members decisively demurred. So pronounced became the opposition to the so-called "revival meetings" that the pastor was constrained to desire that the "quietists," as he termed them, might learn that there were no new kinds of worship, but a more evident manifestation of the old power in a new form. The pastor . . . persevered in his evangelistic program, so that at the close of 1857 he reported that "Many have accepted the experimental knowledge of the truth as it is in Christ Jesus; but there are still others who persist in their 'vain conversation,' provoked by the traditions of the fathers."

Today it does not take long to travel from York, Pennsylvania, to Graceham, Maryland, but the fact that it was an arduous journey in Hagen's day did not deter him from making the trip. He and Kampmann traveled there 13 January 1856, as reported in the *Moravian*, 1/6, 8 February 1856, p. 42, to dedicate a new pulpit. They met at the York depot and traveled by train to Hanover where they were met by

a couple of neat and comfortable green basket-sleighs and were whisked away at a brisk rate, the roads being in excellent sleighing order, and the horses, especially Barney, the Graceham minister's nag, in capital traveling plight. We sometimes marvel how it is that ministers' horses (we have some experience, having had at least six different ones in our own ministerial use and care)—like their purses, wardrobes, pantries, and libraries—though forever doomed to short allowance, "waste not, nor fail." Barney is still a good horse, notwithstanding that he is now 19 years of age and has been used to some purpose by four successive ministers.

The two spent the night in Littlestown and continued the next day

across the Manocasy, through Emmetsburg, toward Graceham (say about twenty-four miles), where we arrived about two o'clock p.m. in the midst of a fearful snowstorm.

Br. and Sr. Ricksecker and children welcomed them. There were two services on Sunday, at which Hagen and Kampmann preached, and another on Monday. Attendance at the services was good, notwithstanding a communicant membership of only 86 and the fact that

all the night long, as on the day before, it stormed and snowed, and sleeted and rained, and froze, rendering for our people the access to the church on the following day very, very difficult.

Hagen did not conduct a revival at Graceham, but his kind of sermonizing pleased the congregation. He returned for the centennial celebration of 8, 9, and 10 October 1858, and he visited the congregation as a member of the P.E.C. 23–28 August 1862, holding daily services, and visiting all members in their homes.

In the meantime, as the Hagen birthday book tells us under the date 31 January 1858, there was the "commencement of an extensive work of grace in the Morav. Church at York P^a." Albright, p. 168, tells us,

> The pastor dedicated two days for complete personal fasting and prayer, that the Holy Spirit might be manifestly poured out upon the congregation. On the following Sunday, his preaching was attended with great spiritual conviction among the people. At the evening service the church was crowded; and many bowed in tears, seeking peace long after the congregation was dismissed.

Why was this occasion noted in the birthday book, which is otherwise devoted exclusively to personal anniversaries? The answer is, I believe, that he recognized this "work of grace" as being a birthday of sorts: the members of the congregation were reborn. At the least, they were very different at his departure in 1861 than they had been when he had arrived in 1855. Hagen had changes ahead of him, too: his Church was in 1857 to separate itself from the Mother Church in Herrnhut, he was to lose his first wife and a stillborn child, and his nation was to pass through a calamitous Civil War.

Levering, *Bethlehem*, p. 731, informs us that Moravian work south of the Lehigh River, across from old Bethlehem, had begun 1 May 1859 in a schoolhouse. In September 1861 it had moved to a grain depot, and

> services were held there with considerable regularity until the close of 1864, principally by the Rev. F. F. Hagen, a member of the Executive Board of the Moravian Church. In that grain-house a congregation was organized on Christmas Day, 1863.

On 22 September 1862 and 28 June 1863 Hagen addressed groups of volunteers who were preparing to go to war. The latter date was just before the Battle of Gettysburg; when that battle was over, everything was different.

Hagen married his second wife, Ellen Smyser of York. He served in Staten Island and New York City, where he was

Francis Florentine Hagen and his boys. The children, from left to right, are probably Willy, Harry, and Ernest. Pruett, who reproduces this picture on p. 10, says that it was taken in Harmony, Iowa, about 1875.

widowed a second time. Two years before Ellen's death, Hagen had moved to New York (1 July 1870); two years afterward (1874), he moved to Harmony, Iowa, taking his three boys with him. From that time there survives a wonderfully evocative photograph of the four of them (Pruett, p. 10). The boots shown in the photograph were necessary, for, as Hagen observed (13 May 1878), "Iowa has a most excellent soil, but a very uncertain climate."

Hagen remained in Harmony for only two or three years, and then began, possibly on his own, to explore the possibilities of starting a Moravian Church in Blairstown, Iowa. A letter to Br. Kluge (21 December 1877) gives us information. Hagen first went there from Poweshick County, Iowa, on Friday, 23 February 1877, preaching there on Saturday and Sunday. He returned to Harmony on 25 May 1877 and 18 August 1877, preaching the next day (Sunday), in German in the morning and in English in the evening, so successfully that after the morning service, several members of the congregation "signified their desire to unite in forming a Moravian Church."

At this awkward moment, Hagen was informed by the P.E.C. that he was retired, but he went back to Blairstown anyhow, and was welcomed by Bro. Lehr. Hagen said later that he had decided to retire there. He set about establishing a congregation, preaching his first sermon on 14 September 1877. "Arrangements have been made with the Evangelical (Albright) congregation for the use of their church, at the rate of $1.50 for each service." Later (on 25 November 1877) the Moravians moved their services to Bryant's Hall, borrowing a pulpit and platform from the Academy in the town. One of Hagen's chief activities seemed to be that of burying children, who were dying of diphtheria, typhoid fever, and spinal meningitis. It was perhaps at this time that Hagen sent Willie, his oldest son, back East, enrolling him in Nazareth Hall. In his 21 December 1877 letter to Br. Kluge, Hagen wrote,

> I am still in a solitary state, sole chef de cuisine and housekeeper. But I am not alone in this thing. I find many students in our excellent Blairstown Academy, and other men, young and old, live alone and board themselves. If this invasion of women's rights becomes too general, I fear it will cause a greater panic among them than their accession to the rights of the ballot-box will among the men.

Hagen preached his farewell sermon at Blairstown in German on 19 May 1878 and visited Harmony, Iowa, 24 May 1878, before starting the long journey back to Bethlehem, where he arrived on 1 June 1878. Then he immediately went to Nazareth to visit Willie, whom he had not seen for two years.

Willie was by this time thirteen, Ernest ten, and Harry eight. It is not clear how Hagen dealt with the two younger boys while he was in Bethlehem. In any event, he stayed with Theodore Wolle for several days before settling (on 6 June 1878) into a dwelling at 33 Centre Street. He made a quick trip to New York in April 1879, but otherwise remained in Bethlehem preaching and substituting, in his spare time arranging a tunebook, composing, translating, writing, and conducting choral groups. He was not to remain there long, however, for in March 1880 he was to be sent to Philadelphia.

In Philadelphia, he kept busy with composing. He assisted various ministers, and became a free-ranging evangelist. While he was resourcefully facing his problems and solving them, the Moravian Church was, without realizing the fact, settling into comfortable and self-satisfied denominational middle age, becoming as static as Hagen was becoming dynamic. The inevitable collision between the static church and the dynamic minister produced a figurative ecclesiastical earthquake that was symbolized by a literal geophysical one. The preliminary groanings were Hagen's revivals, like one that he conducted on 28 October 1883, a flyer for which he pasted into the front of Diary IV.

Hagen's diary implies that the event was not very successful, at least to him personally, for on the day after his sixty-eighth birthday (31 October 1883), he observed,

> Today another year of my life begins. I feel as though I ought to turn over a new leaf & forget that I am a worn-out minister. By the will of others, not by my own, I am a retired minister. I want to be a lion rampant and no longer couchant. Would that I were less of a lion, however, and more like a lamb. The old selflove, which takes offense, resents it, & then gives offense, still crops out when provoked, & leaves regret & unhappiness behind.

There are six sentences in that passage, and they lurch emotionally up and down. The first is merely factual ("another year"), the second rebellious ("a new leaf"), the third acquiescent ("the will of others"), the fourth defiant ("I want to be a lion"), the fifth sober ("would that I were . . . more like a lamb"), and the sixth pathetic ("regret & unhappiness"). Rebellion, as we might have expected, won the day. Subsequently to that event, Hagen wrote in his diary (25 November 1883),

> I moreover prayed to God last Sunday week, when the doctor

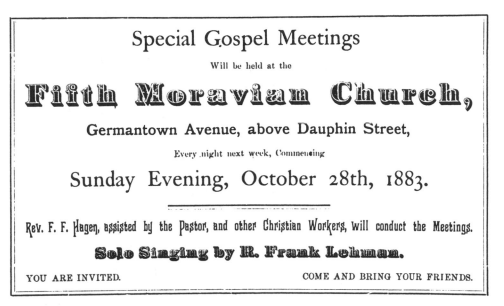

Flyer for a Moravian revival. The original document is pasted into the front of Diary IV.

told me that I had some "brain trouble brewing", that his will be done, and that if . . . I might have a little longer for young children's sake (and also for the gospel's sake), I would try to devote all my remaining time and strength to the cause of revivals and to the religious training of my children. I therefore not only feel bound in the spirit, but also constrained by my Saviour's love to me, and by my love to him, if at all possible, to attend revival meetings at any cost. Ah! for more love and zeal!

Hagen's prayer was spectacularly answered during his return to Salem in 1886 and 1887. Immediately upon arrival in his hometown, he undertook an arduous schedule of preaching and maintained it through a dreadful winter of rain, flood, sleet, snow, and mud, all of which he defied. The most spectacular natural phenomenon that Hagen experienced, however, was an earthquake that occurred in Salem on 31 August 1886. He mentions it casually in his diary: "I left my heart with the Bethania meeting, from which I hope to hear good accounts these days. In the evening 10:30, earthquake."

Hagen's priorities were clear: the Bethania meeting got eighteen words, the earthquake five. Other people's reaction in Salem (2 September 1886) was more excited: "Academy reopened. All the talk for the last 2 days was about the earthquake."

If anything happened on 3, 4, and 5 September Hagen does not note it, but on the 6 September he

> was taken to Friedland with Ernest in Rev. Rondthaler's phaeton by cold river, where a protracted meeting was going on. There was a great earnestness and numbers came forward as penitents. Services a.m., afternoon, and night. Slept in the old parsonage with Ernest. The latter enters heartily into the Spirit of these meetings.

These services continued the next day, conducted by Samuel Augustus Woosley. The Friedberg meetings were still going on when Hagen left (8 September). He was no sooner back in Salem than Ernest was off (9 September) to Macedonia, where another revival was under way. His son attended there until 12 September, and while he was away, yet another meeting commenced (11 September 1886) in the Elm Street Moravian Chapel. This meeting was not to end until Hagen's seventy-first birthday, 30 October 1886, and it was going to shake the church as much as the earthquake had shaken the town. Hagen got much of the credit for the revival, and there were those who would have liked to blame him for the earthquake as well.

The revival continued all the week of 11 September, and Hagen wrote on Saturday, on 18 September, "over 12 persons have found peace and made public profession thereof", on 19 September "Elm Street crowded at 6 p.m., but the service lasted only till 7 and adjourned to the church. Over 60 have risen for prayer up to date. Conversions still take place. Lord, help! to make thy strength perfect in our weakness"; concerning 20–27 September, "Nightly meetings and a growing interest Elm Street"; and for the 27th to the 30th, "Meetings continued at Elm Street & conversions of daily occurrence."

On Friday, 1 October, there was a "large meeting and many seekers and some converts at Elm Street"; on 2 October, "Did not go to Elm Street, but heard that there was a very tender and blessed meeting"; and on 3 October,

> Good preaching morning by Dr. Rondthaler. It is a pity that he sometimes drops his voice too low to be understood. At 3 p.m. a large testimony meeting. . . . Many testified as to what the Lord had done for their souls, and over 20 or 30 rose for prayer. The very brief 6 [o'clock] service was crowded.

On 4 October, "Crowds in attendance. Several testified that they had found peace, and many rose for prayer". On Tuesday, 5 October,

Very large attendance, many seekers, and at the beginning and at the close several professed that their prayers for pardon had been answered. Very many rose for prayer and great earnestness was manifested in prayer. Many young men found peace and are now laboring for souls. Children and young men and women, old hardened sinners, are melted down in godly sorrow at the Saviour's feet. 4th week closed on Friday.

On Sunday, 10 October,

Prayer meeting at 9¾ a.m. in Home Chapel. Excellent testimony-meeting at 3 p.m. in Elm Street, the largest crowd yet, and so all this week many were present and penitents arose every time, and professions of conversion also in every meeting.

On Saturday, 16 October,

Large attendance in the evening.

On Sunday, 17 October,

Experience meeting 3¼ p.m. Very warm meeting. Br. Rondthaler very happy. After 7 o'clock sermon, there was catechetical lecture in the Home Chapel, attended by as many as the room could hold.

On Monday, 18 October,

Large meeting . . . , 11 seekers and 4 professions.

On Saturday, 30 October,

Reached my 71 year, full of gratitude to my patient and longsuffering Lord. Elm Street prayer meeting, the last: 2 rose for prayer.

Now things began to cool a bit, because catechetical classes followed the revival; only when instruction was completed could the converts become communicant Moravians. On 2 November 1886, Hagen reported,

Prayer meeting at 4 every day and confirmation meeting in the evening. The attendance at the latter was large on Sunday but less so in the week. There is comparatively little to draw in catechetical lectures, and earnest people go in order to encourage others to go. The Elm Street meetings were always fully attended to the last, in spite of several fruitless efforts to stop them. Now that they have been colonized over to the big old church it will require another special interposition of Providence (perhaps another earthquake!!) to prevent the devil from having the satisfaction of seeing this good work quenched.

On 14 September, he noted, "In the Salem Church 58 new members were added in the Communion Service 6¾p.m." And so it ended.

Later (30 November 1886), Hagen observed,

A few days ago I gave a small quantity of Canaster to Linda (col^d Meth), at which she exclaimed, "The Lord is my Shepherd, I shall not want!" Her last pipeful of my former supply had just been smoked! The same good old Linda, when I asked her how she felt during the late Earthquake, said, quite excitedly, "Oh! I was so glad! because it's going to be a warning to sinners!" And so it was, even to Salem, who, after 121 years, was in consequence blessed with its first revival!

6
Musician

*H*agen agonized over the fact that when he was trying to meditate and pray, he was distracted by hearing some music that he liked being played elsewhere in the building. After he was scolded by a minister for singing late at night outside a tavern, he defiantly wrote some other compositions. It is easy to infer which pieces of music are involved here, because out of all of Hagen's eighty-one compositions, only four are "pure" music, that is, works unrelated to words: his "Remembrance" Rondoletto (no. 54) and *Scherzo capriccioso* (no. 59), both for piano; his overture for orchestra (no. 51); and his "Florentine" Waltz (no. 25, lost). Everything else that Hagen wrote had texts, and if the texts were not specifically sacred, then they were very moral.

From this it can easily be seen that Hagen interested himself in particular musical media in direct proportion to the extent to which a work could transmit evangelical messages. So the field of music to which he devoted the most expository or polemical writing was hymnody, and there are more organ settings of hymn-tunes (thirty-nine) than of any other kind of piece, and to them can be added the three of his piano solos that are based on hymn-tunes.

Next in importance come his seventeen major anthems, one cantata, six smaller choral pieces, and ten songs with piano, half of which involve a chorus.

Organist's Companion. Cover of hardbound edition.

First I relay what Hagen had to say about music, then I discuss his various kinds of musical performing abilities, and finally I provide a categorical list of his works.

Hagen's taste in gospel tunes may be indicated by those he picked to elaborate in his own settings in the *Organist's Companion,* as follows (the numbers are those of the works as listed in Appendix 3):

ADESTE FIDELES	4	CROSS AND		LENOX	37
ANTIOCH	9	CROWN	22	MARTYN	42
ARLINGTON	10	DUKE STREET	23	MISSIONARY	43
BALERMA	12	FEDERAL		NETTLETON	46
BETHANY	13	STREET	24	NO SORROW	
BOYLSTON	15	"Home, sweet		THERE	47
BRATTLE STREET	16	home"	30	OLD	
CANAAN	17	HURSLEY	32	HUNDREDTH	50
CONSOLATOR	20	I'M A PILGRIM	33	PLEYEL'S HYMN	52
CORONATION	21	LABAN	36	REST FOR THE	

Hagen also arranged three church tunes for piano: "Am I a soldier of the Cross" (no. 6); "I'm a pilgrim" (no. 34, but actually an arrangement of the organ setting, or vice versa); and "There'll be no more sorrow there" (no. 72). These and the two works mentioned at the beginning of this chapter comprise his entire output for piano.

Hagen was able to play the piano and organ by the age of twelve, apparently having learned the art at the Salem Boys School. Most organ music of his time was merely piano music that was not impossible to play on the organ, but Hagen distinguishes idiomatically between the two. He furthered his piano-playing skills at Nazareth Hall, possibly under the guidance of

Organist's Companion. Cover of periodical edition.

Johann Christian Bechler, and at some point he also learned to play the violin.

Hagen's taste in what he would have called "uncommitted" music is indicated in part by the works he arranged for this same publication: eleven by Batiste; nine by Beethoven; eight each by Mendelssohn and Wagner; six by Rossini; five by Rubinstein; four each by Handel, Rinck, and Schubert; three each by Bach, Gounod, Pinsuti, and Verdi (with one by Bach-Gounod); two by Franz Joseph Haydn; and one each by André, Arne, Bord, Scotson Clark, Flotow, Gluck, Michael Haydn, Heller, Kreutzer, Leybach, Lvoff, Mozart, Schumann, Soder-mann, Stradella, Valenti, Voss, and Weber.

I have found few contemporaneous descriptions of Hagen's organ playing. "A Brother" wrote to *The Moravian*, 1/2, 11 January 1856, p. 9, to describe "The Centennial Jubilee of the Moravian Church at York, Pa., on the 19th and 20th of December, 1855." Three meetings were carried out by Bishop Wolle and Brethren Kampmann and Samuel Reinke. The Bishop read Hagen's history of the congregation, which was published in *The Moravian*, 1/1, 1 January 1856, p. 1. There had been a preliminary solemn prayer meeting to close the first century, and the celebration commenced on the 19th. "A Brother" writes,

> On entering the church, I was delighted with hearing the rich tones of a new organ that has just been purchased by the congregation and was fitted up in time for this joyful occasion. Both the sweetness of the instrument and the taste of its player (who was no other than the minister of the church, Brother Hagen) were fully developed in the various meetings of this and the following day, and added much—as every lover of music will know—to the fervent and happy expression of devotional feeling and praise.

Hagen provided an article "Church Music" in the *Moravian* I, on 19 September 1856, p. 300. He begins by asserting that "Moravian church music yields to no other in point of devotional effect." He divided the music into "two styles, the *choral* or psalmodical, and the *rhythmical*."

> The choral style is most generally used in our churches, because a slow movement is best adapted for congregational singing, and besides, when correctly executed, productive of magnificent effect. . . . When in slow choral tunes the air is sung by all in unison or octaves, and the other parts entirely left away, the effect is impaired and becomes rather meagre. And it is for this reason that more rapid rhythmical movements—we mean lively and popular airs (such as "Sing Hallelujah," &c., page 145, Wolle's tune book)—are generally preferred to dull, drawling

and monotonous choral-tunes, in such communities especially where musical science and correct organ and melodeon playing still belong to the category of pia desiderata. . . . One of our home missionaries in the Blue Ridge mission field . . . found it necessary, whenever he would obtain congregational singing, . . . to fall in with the native rhythmical style, by non-connoisseurs falsely styled methodist tunes. These tunes, both at the South and West, are common to nearly all the different churches, and they constitute, rude and unscientific as they are, the household-tunes of that people, to which they cling with the same fondness as we do to ours.

Our tunes are essentially German, and many of them are national church tunes . . . but, however natural and beautiful German choral singing may seem to ourselves, . . . yet it would be . . . difficult to introduce them into some parts of English America. . . . Some of our most beautiful hymns . . . cannot be sung to any of the popular American metres. . . .

From patriotic (in the Moravian sense) and musical considerations, we would strongly advocate the cultivation of our own peculiar psalmody; . . . we protest against . . . enthusiastic ultraism . . . which refuses to identify Moravianism with any other combination of sounds than those in Gregor's, Latrobe's, and Wolle's tune books, and affects a dislike bordering on disgust for all other tunes.

. . . Our rhythmical church-compositions, or choir-music . . . require some skill to perform . . . and are moreover reserved for special occasions by select choirs. . . . When preaching and hearing are not the principal thing, then congregational singing may, very properly, be relieved by rhythmical performances by the choir. . . . These festive services and liturgies produce a very pleasing impression, even upon persons who have no religious principles whatever.

Hagen's involvement in hymnody has not been previously noticed. His scrapbook contains a letter that he wrote to the *Moravian*, evidently before the 1878 Synod (I have not located the original publication).

Much care and labor have recently been bestowed on our English Hymn-Book. Many defects have been supplied, and several improvements made by the omission of old hymns and the introduction of new ones.

Now that the old hymn-book has been so greatly changed, it seems to be the proper time to think of publishing a new tune-book to correspond with it.

Besides the chorales to which our hymns are sung, we need a larger variety of original Moravian and other anthems and choruses; and also some of the best and most popular pieces of American psalmody. . . .

There is a divinely inspired music or tone-language, which expresses the sentiment of hymns, with even more pathos and power than the choicest words. The old masters excelled in this species of musical composition.

Still, I venture to assert, that the gift (charisma) of composing new sacred music has not been entirely taken away from the Church, as the gift of working miracles is said to have been.

It is both wise and safe to apply to old and to new music . . . the Apostolic precept: "Prove all things, and hold fast to that which is good." Now this . . . is just what I propose should be done at this time in the matter of Moravian Church music.

My reasons for editing a new Tune Book, are:

1. There are tunes in Bro. Peter Wolle's book, which have become useless ever since the new hymn-book has dropped the hymns to which they exclusively belong. By dropping such tunes . . . we may gain room for others which are much needed, for we have new hymns to which there are no tunes whatever in the old book.

2. In the present book, the key or pitch of some chorales is so high as to cause their execution to be very difficult. The singing of the congregation becomes pitifully faint, uncertain, and discordant. . . .

3. A revision of the counterpoint is also important.

Our Tune-Book needs many changes, and if the right ones are made—and we have the material from which it can be done—it will rank as high among works of sacred psalmody, as our hymn-book . . . does among other hymn-books.

A word about the so-called "Gospel Hymns," which are now sung in every nook and corner of the world, where English and American voices sing. They have had a glorious and successful mission. They have proved to be a mine of spiritual profit to those who have devoutly used them, and also of no little pecuniary profit to those who deal in this popular publication. The rapidity of its spread, and the universality of its use are among the marvels of the age.

But the taste for this style of sacred music, in spite of its present popularity, is necessarily ephemeral. It will not be long before American music will have emerged from its present elementary condition, and American worshipers will acquire sufficient taste and skill to execute devotional music, such as correct classical taste can approve.

Could not the coming Synod be prevailed upon to give the subject of a new Tune-Book some attention? . . . It strikes me to be well to publish, in the first place, a book containing all the tunes which the new Hymn-Book calls for. Another book should contain a collection of anthems and choruses. . . .

There is a fund of original manuscript Church music, never before printed, in the Musical Repertory of the venerable church at Bethlehem, Pa., on which the compiler might draw to excellent purpose.

Ought we not to make the attempt to preserve to ourselves and to others, these precious musical treasures? The existence of a Moravian tune, anthem, and chorus book would stimulate in all our churches new efforts to cultivate taste for good Church music, and at the same time a spirit of grateful praise to our blessed God and Saviour. . . .

For years I have wished for a good, printed collection of Moravian Church music; and have even made some experiments as to the practicability of supplying with English texts, some of our best old original German Moravian compositions. I am glad to find that the pastors of the church at Bethlehem, our excellent organist—Prof. Theodore F. Wolle—and Bro. E. F. Bleck, organist emeritus, who had been my revered music-teacher, when I was a pupil at Nazareth Hall, 50 years ago—hold similar views as to our present musical needs; and I doubt not that many others do. . . .

This interesting letter reveals two facets of Hagen's musical tastes. First, as early as 1878, long before anyone else, he was presciently calling for the publication of the music in the Moravian archives. The first editions were not to be produced until 1939, under the editorship of Hans T. David, and not until 1956 was the Moravian Music Foundation created for the comprehensive preservation, cataloging, study, and publication of the heritage.

Second, Hagen reveals a contrasting appreciation of Gospel hymns. In a letter to the *Moravian,* written from Brooklyn, Iowa (29 May 1877), he further explains his position.

I have an impression . . . that the peculiar style of music in Moody and Sankey's Gospel Hymns, now in universal use all over the Far West, . . . has the effect, on the one hand, of *subduing* very loud manifestations of strong emotional feeling; and on the other, of moving, in a gentle and tender way, the cold, unfeeling hearts of the formalists and hardened sinners. I hear that some of our people in the East refuse to sing Moody and Sankey hymns! I admit that the music thereof is very easy and in keeping with the present elementary grade of American musical taste and culture—and therefore so widely popular. But even cultivated singers, and such as have been accustomed to the classically beautiful German chorales of our Moravian Hymnbook, can get a blessing when they sing Moody and Sankey hymns; and they will if their hearts are in tune. Out of the abundance of the heart, the mouth speaks, in any language, or makes melody unto the Lord, according to any tune, whether old or new. Let no one therefore be afraid of revivals, or of Gospel hymns; but, rather, let us all pray without ceasing, and in everything give thanks.

Hagen kept persistently at the idea of a new tunebook. The
Bethlehem Times used to publish full accounts of the actions of
Moravian synods, even when they took place in distant locations. That of 1878 occurred in Hope, Indiana, and the fifth
day's proceedings (14 October) included Hagen's memorial
(i.e., proposal), read by W. H. Rice,

> which was a very effective and interesting appeal, that synod
> authorize the publication of a new Moravian tune book as also of
> an anthem and chorus book for the use of schools and families.

If the Synod had approved, then the equivalent of the Moravian Music Foundation would have been founded by Hagen in
1878, not by a confederation of Friends in 1956.

The tenth day's proceedings were much concerned with
music:

> The music by the church choir, under the direction of Prof.
> Albrecht, was all that could be asked for. The alto and soprano
> duet by the Misses Jennie and Anna R. Holland was very finely
> rendered. The alto voice of Miss Jennie Holland is one of rare
> richness and compass. . . .
>
> Report of the Committee on Publications was called up and
> elicited quite a lively discussion. The following resolutions were
> presented.
>
> Resolved, that the early publication of an anthem and tune
> book be referred to the P. E. C.
>
> Resolved, that we recommend to P. E. C. that Bro. F. F. Hagen
> be the compiler and the brethren Massa Warner, Theodore Wolle,
> James Beck, E. G. Close, H. A. Brickenstein, C. B. Schultz, H. A.
> Jacobson, and Frederick Albreacht a committee of revision. . . .
>
> Mr. C. A. Luckenbach wanted to know whether there was any
> expense connected with this which the church would have to
> pay.
>
> Rev. J. Blickensderfer replied that the agent of publications
> assured him that the work would pay for itself.
>
> Mr. Luckenbach could not see the use of changing our tunes;
> there was no difficulty experienced in Bethlehem congregation in
> singing.
>
> Rev. W. H. Rice said we had a beautiful new hymnbook, au-
> thorized by the highest authority, but not tunes to all the hymns
> in the book.
>
> Mr. Luckenbach doubted it, and had never met with any such.
>
> Mr. Rice begged to be handed a hymnbook to enlighten the
> brother from Bethlehem.
>
> Mr. Luckenbach begged the brother from Nazareth not to be-
> come excited.
>
> Rev. Rice: I am not excited! I am only too glad that the brother

has brought up this issue. (A hymnbook having been found, he opened it and read) "Nearer my God to thee," &c. There is no tune in our tune book to which this can be sung.

Mr. Luckenbach: If I mistake not, that hymn is frequently sung at Bethlehem, with full organ accompaniment.

Rev. E. J. Regennas: Our organist has gone to a great deal of trouble and has provided a book of tunes for himself.

Rev. Kampmann said that it is a matter of importance. The whole point lies in what Bro. Luckenbach said, who will foot the bill? Desirable as a new tunebook is, can the Church pay for it or can it not?

Rev. Clewell: If organists were here they would immediately say, "By all means let us have a new tunebook."

Rev. [Henry J.] Van Vleck: I think it well to have a new tune book. With all respect to the compiler of the book now in use, I must say that the tunes as arranged are so high as to be reached only by larks, let alone human beings.

Rev. Klose: . . . It is the highest time to have such a publication. The idea is not to do away with our tunes but to reintroduce some old and beautiful melodies. The expense will be trifling. . . . The point of Bro. Van Vleck is well taken.

Rev. Kluge strongly favored it.

Mr. C. A. Luckenbach backed down from his position, and the resolution was adopted unanimously, though the summary for the fourteenth day includes Rev. Prof. Schulze's complaint that

> When an English hymnbook is wanted, even at the risk of thousands of dollars, the venture is at once made. When a new English tune-book is suggested, the request is forthwith granted. When we ask for a German Sunday school hymnbook and 800 copies are subscribed for in advance, it cannot be done. It is very peculiar that nothing can be a success that is issued in German.

Hagen evidently set immediately to work, for his diary tells us (20 April 1879) that he was "busy writing all the week. Progressed with the new tunebook as far as T. 185." His diary (26 November 1883) tells us, "I remained at home nearly all the week busily employed with preparing copy for a hymnbook." I do not know what became of his work, though it may have become part of the hymnal that was used in the United States from 1909 to 1969.

Conducting fascinated Hagen. His granddaughter, Mary Hagen Mills (Mrs. Oscar E.), reports:

> During Grandfather's stay in New York City, he sang in the musical organization of which Leopold Damrosch, father of the late Walter Damrosch, was director.

Hagen must have been involved with the Bethlehem Philharmonic in some way or another, since his Overture in F (no. 51),
one of the first orchestral overtures to be composed in the
United States, is dedicated to that body. He wrote competently
and idiomatically for the various instruments, both in that
work and in his large concert anthems, the accompaniments of
which also require an orchestra.

On 25 December 1882, Hagen "heard Beethoven's mass . . .
in St. Clement's Church, Cherry and 20th"; and on 27 January
1883, he "heard Redemption by Gounod, performed by Cece-
lian (400 voices) and Theo. Thomas' Orch. (60 pieces). Very fine
and edifying also." Hagen often uses the term *edifying* in connection with critical comments on sermons or musical performances; it is clear that what he meant was that an "edifying"
event gave his mind something to occupy it. Sometimes he
suspected that some events would not be edifying; in those
cases he stayed home and grimly noted the fact in his diary.

Hagen did a surprisingly large amount of conducting, in
both churches and concert halls, sometimes initiating the
group himself. On 10 November 1870, for example, he "made a
futile attempt at commencing a German choir for Olivet
Chapel." By 17 November, however, he had got it going.

During his 1878–1880 stay in Bethlehem, Hagen conducted a
group called Concordia, which serenaded J. Seaman when he
left for Colorado (4 May 1879), and (13 May 1879) Br. Bachman,
who had preached his farewell sermon on 11 May 1879. In
addition to serenades, the group also gave public performances, such as on 7 February 1880, the occasion of a "Concordia
concert in Moravian Hall, well attended."

While working with this group, Hagen wrote a letter (19 June
1879) to the editor of the *Daily Times*, pleading for the organiza-
tion of a Choral Union or Oratorio Society in Bethlehem.

> A chorus of at least 100 singers who have sufficient knowledge
> and skill for being drilled into a respectable performance of
> Handel's, Haydn's, Mozart's, Mendelssohn's, and even Richard
> Wagner's most popular choruses, could readily be obtained from
> our various church choirs, select musical societies, schools and
> social circles, in Old and South Bethlehem. There is, in fact, more
> and better vocal and instrumental material in our town for the
> formation of a good musical society than ever before, even in its
> best musical days. All that is needed is concentration, drill, and
> patient, enthusiastic, intelligent, and loving work.
>
> The compositions of the old masters . . . are not difficult . . .
> and when rendered intelligently and with proper expression, are
> as effective and enjoyable to correct musical taste as any other

kind of music. Modern acrobatic performances, with which prima donnas, and virtuosi on the piano, violin, or cornet astonish the natives, are not the only good music in the land. . . .

Our venerable Philharmonic Society, Mr. E. Ricksecker's Amateur Orchestra, the Frohsinn, the youthful Concordia might furnish excellent instrumental as well as vocal aid to an enterprise of this kind, without the least injury to their own interests. . . .

I do not know if such a group actually came into existence, but sometimes Hagen was asked to take charge elsewhere as a guest conductor, as for instance on 20 September 1879, when he went to Hazleton, Pennsylvania, and stayed at Br. Bartel's, evidently to lead the Choral Society in that town on 15 October 1879 (first rehearsal, 1 October 1879).

He describes (11 February 1880) a more unusual involvement:

Commenced (after service in the Church) with a new Singing Club of colored gentlemen in Fry's Barbershop opposite Eagle Hotel! Going into the Minstrel business! But they show as much aptness for the divine art as anybody and very strong musical impulses. They sing and perform with strong emphasis and fervor.

His most exciting guest involvement began on 14 January 1887, when he "was requested to take charge of the Philharmonic Society" (Salem), his first rehearsal occurring on 18 January. On 1 February 1887 he wrote: "The Philharmonic rehearsal excited me so much that I cannot go to sleep for a long time, owing to the blood-burdened state of my poor brain!" On 4 February he noted: "Drilled the solo singers in the Music Hall."

On 1 March 1887 Hagen wrote: "Practiced quartettes at Mr. Ebert's." On March 7: "Practiced with Mr. Ebert at his house Schubert's *Wanderer.*" On March 24: "Concert (Academy) receipts $45. Much troubled with vertigo." And on 21 April 1887: "Concert for the benefit of the Temperance Club at Winston. Conducted."

The Bernard J. Pfohl Collection, book 2, provides in manuscript the program for the concert given at Academy Chapel on 24 March 1887:

1. Prayer. Solos & Chorus. *Moses in Egypt.* Society & Orchestra. Rossini.
2. Cantata. *On Shore & Sea.* Sullivan. Accompanist. Miss Van

Vleck. Solos: Miss A. Meinung, Mrs. Heller [Keller?], Mrs.
Ebert, Messrs. Lichtenthaler & Vogler.

3. Flute solo. "Tis the last rose of summer." Mrs. D. S. Butner.
Accompanist: Miss Van Vleck.
4. Song. *The Wanderer.* F. Schubert. Mr. E. A. Ebert.
5. Serenade. F. Schubert. Solo: Mr. F. H. Vogler. Orchestral accompaniment.
6. Quartette. "Brave Grenadiėr." Jansen. For male voices with basso solo.
7. *Cujus animam. Stabat Mater.* Rossini. Solo: Mr. A. Lichtenthaler, Orchestral accompaniment.
8. Solo & Chorus. "Inflammatus." Rossini. Solo, Mrs. Heller, Orchestral accompaniment.
9. Quartette for mixed voices (English style). Hatton. Mrs. Ebert. Miss Carmichael. Messrs. Vogler & Ebert.
10. "The judgment of the elect." *Mors et vitae.* Soprano solo: Mrs. Ebert. Baritone: Mr. Ebert. Chorus: female voices. Chorale: Full chorus & orchestra.

The concert was repeated in Brown Opera House, Winston, on 12 April 1887, sponsored by the Twin City Reform Club, with additional violin solos by Robert L. Carmichael.

According to information in the Pfohl Collection, Hagen apparently served as conductor during a temporary absence of George Markgraff, who preceded and followed Hagen's brief tenure. After the two performances in 1887, the group began work on Romberg's "The lay of the bell," with the hope of performing it "before summer," but the performance is not specifically recorded in the minutes. In a long and detailed article, "Fifty-five Years with the Moravian Band," *Twin City Sentinel,* Winston-Salem, N. C., published 4 May 1935 on the occasion of the fiftieth anniversary of the combination of the two cities, Pfohl reports,

About 1858 Salem Classical Music Society was formed, for the purpose of rendering oratorios and other choral works with orchestral accompaniment. The building north of the Wachovia Historical Society was erected, the upper story was fitted up for the Society, a small but well adapted hall for the work of that day. Rev. F. F. Hagen, Rev. M. E. Grunert and Mr. E. W. Leinbach were the leaders in carrying on the new work. . . . Encouraged by Rev. F. F. Hagen, in 1888, at Commencement, Handel's "Samson" was given. Mendelssohn's "St. Paul" followed the next year.

Hagen was extremely competent as a composer. It is surprising that he was able to produce as much music as he did, in view of his other varied and extensive involvements. His grandson tells us:

> While in York, advanced in years, with sight and hearing seriously impaired, he composed church anthems without the aid of any musical instrument. According to my father, some of these anthems were used by the choir of the York First Moravian Church. Grandfather was gifted with a musical ear of "perfect pitch" which stood him in good stead.

I went to York to hunt for these pieces, but found nothing. However, they may be hidden among his undated works, included in the following categorical list that completes mention in this chapter of all of Hagen's compositions (see the initial chronology for the dated works). Note that Hagen was primarily interested in choral music, and that he almost invariably attached a chorus even to his songs.

Anthems

1.	"And I heard a voice from heaven"	7
2.	"And the seventh angel"	8
3.	"Bis dereinst mein Stündlein schlägt"	14
4.	"God is our refuge"	26
5.	"Herr wie sind deine Werke so gross und viel"	29
6.	"How amiable are thy tabernacles"	31
7.	"Kyrie eleison"	35
8.	"Lift up your heads, O ye gates"	38
9.	"Lobsinget Gott"	40
10.	"Lord, let thy blest angelic bands"	41
11.	"O delightful theme"	49
12.	"Praise waiteth for thee"	53
13.	"Schlaf, liebes Kind"	60
14.	"Sel'ge Lebensstunden"	61
15.	"Siehe, ich verkündige euch grosse Freude"	63
16.	"Unto the Lamb that was slain"	74
17.	"Ye are come unto Mt. Zion"	80

Cantata

1.	*Christmas Cantata*	19

Smaller Choral Pieces

1.	"Ach, bleib' mit deiner gnade"	3

Songs with Piano

7
Evening Song

S *unset* was a long time coming to Hagen, and it did not come easily. During his long life, mostly after the age of sixty, he suffered from strokes, vertigo, colds, lumbago, bronchitis, sciatica, malaria, sprained foot, broken ankle, and rheumatism. His prayers for a little more time originated not in a fear of death but only because he had young children to care for and much work to do. Illness never stopped him, but only rechanneled his energies. His troubles were merely something over which to triumph. John F. Hagen tells us in his "Memories,"

> Later Grandfather came to live with us at Lititz, Pa., full of years, but nonetheless brave in spirit and active in mind.

Auto-Biography

> An accident by which 3 ribs were fractured confined me to bed 6 weeks & utterly unfitted me for work. P.E.C. put me in the retire list & sent Rev. W. Hoch to Harmony.

Apparently this accident occurred in 1877, for Henry J. Van Vleck writes in the Gnadenhutten, Ohio, diary (19 September 1877), as reported by Wetzel, "received an unexpected and mysterious letter from Rev. F. F. Hagen, who has been retired,

The mature Francis Florentine Hagen. John Francis Hagen, in "Some memories . . . ," says that Hagen had "a very high forehead, short beard, full mustache, and bushy side-burns. He laughed with his eyes, which often flashed with deep earnestness. He was meticulous in dress, smoked a large pipe, and carried a gold-headed cane. He loved a good meal and drank an occasional beer. He greeted everyone on the street, whether stranger or friend." Pruett uses this picture as his frontispiece, and it was published in Albright opposite p. 168.

is without home, etc., etc." Hagen wanted Van Vleck to find a home for him in Gnadenhutten. The pastor tried, not only in his own congregation but also in those of Joseph J. Ricksecker (Sharon) and of C. C. Lanius (Dover, First), but he was unsuccessful.

Auto-Biography

After being somewhat reinvigorated, I accepted an invitation from Br. Enos Lehr, formerly of Bethlehem Pa, to come to Blairstown & try to form a church. A little flock was soon gathered, but as its permanency required the presence of an able minister, I was relieved. I returned to Bethlehem weak & worn by the rough climate. I left the work in better hands.

The rest of my life is soon told. As far as I was able I gladly assisted other ministers, whenever called upon, mainly in Palmyra & Riverside, N.J., & in the 4th and 5th churches in Philadelphia. I was finally sent for, while residing in 1319 Green St., Philad. Pa, to come to York in 1893 to aid Br. Robert Herbst, who had consumption, in his arduous City Mission work. In 1894 I had a severe fall, which lamed me for life, after I had lain in the York Hospital for three long months with a broken right thigh or hip bone. I was discharged as cured but with a lame leg, for life, just like my sainted father. Again, in 1897, I had another fall, nearly fatal thro concussion of the brain, which broke my left arm, deafened me in the ear, shattered my musical nerves, so that the finest music is a discordant noise. Music was my idol, but it has been dashed to pieces. Nor am I able to understand preaching any more. And now I am awaiting a final resolution of all things.

Meanwhile, while there is any vitality left, I will show the Lord's death, waiting the time when the Lord will call me to himself. But I am happy in a conscious sense of his love.

Next month, Oct. 30th, if the Lord spare my life, I will be 86 years old. Praise & prayer & thanksgiving should employ my remaining days, until the Lord calls me to himself.

Affectionately inscribed for my dear friend & Brother in Christ, J. L. Kable & Arny Pauli, with love to all the brethren, by F. F. Hagen.

On 17 October 1882, Hagen reports in his diary, in very shaky penciled lines (all the diaries are otherwise in ink), "Took sick. Serious effusion on the brain. I am weak, whilst I am writing to my son Ernest. Dr Minich attended me." This was a stroke, and it was succeeded by vertigo and weakness. Finally he went out 29 October, the day before his sixty-seventh birthday, having become ambulatory in less than two weeks.

On 24 June 1883 Hagen writes: "Sick for over two weeks during this month with sciatica and malaria." On 26 November 1883. "Several attempts at going out were attended by considerable vertigo, so that I did not venture far from home." He kept himself busy there, however. Though Hagen was indeed subjected to a whole panoply of illnesses, that circumstance did not force his retirement: First, the P.E.C. gave the order, and second, being bedridden or housebound merely gave Hagen an opportunity to translate this or compile that. He suffered enormously, but he never gave in to sickness: it was as if he consisted essentially of pure mind and spirit, his body and its ills being merely an annoying encumbrance.

On 3 December 1883, he wrote:

> A series of gospel services having been appointed in the 4th church, I attended in the evening, for I reasoned thus: a clot on the brain, which is my present danger, may come at home, yea, in my bed, as well as in a prayer meeting, and if I am to choose between dying while laboring for Christ in a prayer meeting, or while I am from fear of death staying at home doing nothing, I would choose death in a prayer meeting, not because there is the least merit in the latter mode of dying, but because we should always have our loins girded and our lamplight burning. . . . It was a cold evening to ride from Callowhill to Dauphin and back, but it did not harm me. I pray that God may spare me to go again tomorrow evening.

He did go to the prayer meeting the following evening, and the night after that (5 December 1883) he even preached himself.

> I felt no ill effects of my effort today, altho' some said that it would be the death of me if I preached too much. I would rather die of preaching than of doing nothing.

In the course of December 1883, Hagen's handwriting in the diaries began to deteriorate almost into illegibility. Apparently he also looked quite sick. He mentions one lady as repeatedly wishing him a "Happy New Year— a *whole* year"; and his landlady made him move closer to her, so that she could listen for him, in case he needed help. He himself believed that he was dying, and he spent several weeks in determined efforts (which kept going wrong) to get court approval of Br. W. A. Rice as guardian for his children. By February 1884, however, Rice was too ill to conduct services, and Hagen was filling in for him, preaching (3 February 1884) on Philippians 1:21, "For me to live is Christ, and to die is gain." The previous 25 November, Hagen had written in his diary,

> I am in a strait betwixt two, having a desire to depart to be with Christ, which is far better; nevertheless to abide with my children is more needful for them. If I live in the flesh, this is the fruit of my labor: care for my young boys; yet what I shall choose, I wot not. To me to live is Christ and to die is gain. [At this point he sounds almost suicidal, but he had nearly a quarter-century of productive life before him.]

On 28 February 1884, Hagen noted that his room was so cold that he caught bronchitis. He moved to another room, and his writing again deteriorated, this time even more badly than before, finally ceasing altogether through June, July, and August. Suddenly, on 31 August 1884, there was a two-word entry, "Brethren's Festival," and the following day the diary was resumed in a strong and youthful hand. He had made an amazing recovery, and, while he was confined to his quarters, he had kept himself busy.

On 5 October 1884, however, he records, quite casually, "Sprained my foot and was confined to the house for three weeks." On 2 November 1884 he writes: "I have been able to go out again, but am much distressed by vertigo. Was very busy translating into German during the past weeks the text to M. Arban's *Complete Method for the Cornet à Pistons.*" He does not say why he was doing so, but the obvious reason is that his son Harry had an interest in such instruments.

Hagen sometimes covers a whole month at one sitting. He did so in July 1884, and he was becoming cranky.

> Commenced the month with a bad cold, lumbago, &c. The fourth of July passed off as disagreeably as usual. Bethlehem's Sunday School pic-nic on the 8th did not put me to any inconvenience: I did not attend it. On the 8th, Rev. Mr. Hoch from Phil[a] was here and uttered sentiments which I could only reply to by telling him that I stood in doubts of his conversion.

In Hagen's day, doctors' prescriptions were not mixed by pharmacists; the physician either supplied the nostrums or instructed the patient to buy the ingredients and mix them himself. Hagan had suffered a stroke and on 25 November 1883 he received a warning that:

> there was a new brain-trouble brewing and that I must be careful. An oz. of Bromide of Potassium, dissolved in ½ coffee cup of water, 1 teaspoon after every meal and before going to bed.

Hagen evidently gained so much experience with illness and medicine that he began to feel qualified to prescribe medicine. On 6 December 1883, he reported,

> Br. Rice preached in the 4th Church. Good attendance and sermon to the purpose. I took charge of the "after meeting" at Br. Ricksecker's request, who is troubled with malarial sensations! I advised him yesterday to take a large dose of quinine, 10 grains at a time.

Hagen's prescription did not work, because on the following day, in the service, Ricksecker handed Hagen a note saying that he was too ill to continue, and asked Hagen to take over. Hagen did, and offered to keep the services going for the remaining days.

Hagen was also capable of confusing his medicines, as we learn on 2 May 1886: "Took sick in the night from taking carbon-lead instead of zinc."

Pruett, on p. 11, corrects the widely circulated statement contained in the biographical notes of Dickinson's *Early American Moravian Church Music* octavos to the effect that Hagen suffered a broken hip in 1870 that forced him to retire from the ministry. Pruett says that the correct date is 1877, but according to Hagen,

Auto-Biography

> Last of all in 1893 [in the other copy he says 1894] I aided Br. Robert Herbst who was suffering from consumption, but the following year I fractured my right hip, & after lying in York Hospital for three months was discharged as cured but with a lame leg, for life, just like my sainted father. . . . I am now nearly 86 years old, and waiting the time when the Lord will call me to himself. But I am happy in a conscious sense of his love.

So the correct date is 1893 or 1894. Mary Hagen (Mrs. Oscar E.) Mills reports in "Some memories. . . ,"

> Grandfather lived with my late father, Rev. Ernest S. Hagen, D.D., and family at Lititz, Penn'a, during his last few years. He was almost totally deaf and blind & also quite lame from an accident.
>
> It was my duty to carry & fetch his meal tray upstairs & I received many a dime for doing that. Every morning I had to read (or shout) the Daily Texts to him. He had an octagonal-

Abend-Lied (Evening Song), no. 48. This is Hagen's last datable work (November 1898). The text is "Nun lege ich mich schlafen" ("Now I lay me down to sleep").

shaped wooden wall clock which hung over his desk & which he would take down from its nail many times every day to "feel" what time it was. The figures were practically all worn off. Every now & then he would get the idea that the clock was "out of fix" & would shake it or pound on the desk with it. Of course he couldn't hear it when he put his ear to it.

Then he would call me to take it to the jeweler's to be repaired. It was repaired many times, but finally, after so much rough treatment, it just wouldn't run any more. But he still called for me to take it to be repaired. Then I used to keep it downstairs for several days & then take it back to him. He was satisfied, because he thought it was running again. For that service I received many a quarter!

Mrs. Mills' father, E. S. Hagen, wrote an obituary, the closing paragraph of which follows:

In March 1902 he came to Lititz and spent the remainder of his days with his son, the pastor of the Moravian Congregation, enjoying good health up to four weeks ago, when he began visibly to fail. After being confined to his bed but for one week, he fell asleep in Jesus on Sunday evening July 7, 1907, having reached the age of 91 years, 8 months, and 7 days. The funeral services were held on Wednesday afternoon, July 10, 1907, in the Church, and were in charge of Bro. C. D. Kreider. The Brn. T. W. Shields of York, Pa. and S. J. Blum of Nazareth Hall and Paul de Schweinitz of Bethlehem delivered addresses. The choir sang the Morning Star. Interment was made in the Old Graveyard, No. 1237.

Appendix 1
Publications of
"Morning Star"

The various texts and tunes involved in the complex of material could be called "Morgenstern" (original text incipit), MORGENSTERN (original tune name), "Morning Star" (text incipit of all English translations), HAGEN (name assigned to Hagen's tune), or any one of a number of translations into other languages. I have elected to use the name "Morning Star" in all references.

A section of the following résumé is devoted to each different text of "Morning Star" and each different tune to which the words were set. The sections occur in chronological order. When a text and a tune have the same date, the text comes first.

It was not possible in the time available to discover every publication of the many tunes and translations. I solicit additions to the list, and request that these be provided in the form of a machine copy of the publication title page and of the pertinent pages. These will be acknowledged in the *Moravian Music Journal* as they are received.

Text of 1657

Johannes Scheffler ("Angelus Silesius") *Heilige Seelenlust Oder Geistliche Hirten-Lieder.* . . , Breslaw [the official approval for publication is dated 1 May 1657], vol. 1, no. 26.

Sie will das Jesulein als den wahren Morgenstern
in dem Himmel ihres Herzens haben

1. Morgenstern der finstern Nacht,
   Der die Welt voll Freuden macht,
       Jesulein,
       Komm herein,
   Leucht in meines Herzens Schrein.

2. Schau, dein Himmel ist in mir,
   Er begehrt dich, deine Zier.
       Säum dich nicht,
       O mein Licht,
   Komm, komm, eh der Tag anbricht.

3. Deines Glanzes Herrlichkeit
   Übertrifft die Sonne weit,
       Du allein,
       Jesulein,
   Bist, was tausend Sonnen sein.

4. Du erleuchtest alles gar,
   Was jetzt ist und kommt und war.
       Voller Pracht
       Wird die Nacht,
   Weil dein Glanz sie angelacht.

5. Deinem freudenreichen Strahl
   Wird gedienet überall.
       Schönster Stern
       Weit und fern
   Ehrt man dich wie Gott, den Herrn.

6. Ei nun, güldnes Seelenlicht,
   Komm herein und säum dich nicht.
       Komm herein,
       Jesulein,
   Leucht in meines Herzens Schrein.

Source: Hans Ludwig Held (ed.), *Angelus Silesius sämtliche poetische Werke*. München, 1949, vol. 2, p. 69, courtesy Henry Williams, Moravian College, Bethlehem.

"Morgenstern" is among those Scheffler works to which Mearns accorded "a very high place in German hymns," and it was also among those chosen by Zinzendorf. I have been unable to locate a copy of Scheffler's original hymnal, but the first of the six stanzas is transmitted by Zahn (1852), and all of them by Held. The text has the unique rhythm 7.7.3.3.7. trochaic.

Subsequent Publications

1741. *Christliches Gesang-Buch der Evangelischen Brüder-Gemeinen von 1735*, 3d ed., n.p., 1741, p. 284.
    This is the earliest Moravian publication of Scheffler's text. Major changes were as follows. Stanza 1: "finstern" became "finstre." 2: omitted. 5(4): "Weit" became "nah." 6(5): "Güldnes" became "wahres."

1753. *Etwas vom Liede Moses . . . Alt- und neuer Brüder-Gesang*, London, 1753, p. 466, no. 819.

1783. *Gesangbuch, zum Gebrauch der evangelischen Brüdergemein*, Barby, 1783, p. 40, no. 79 ("Mel. 310"). Major alterations were as follows. Stanzas 2 and 4 were omitted. 5(3): "Wird gedienet" became "folgt man willig."
    P. 285, no. 541 ("Mel. 203") presents another text that begins "Morgenstern!" but is in another rhythm.

1862. Scheffler, *Werke*, Regensburg, vol. 1, p. 63.

1891. *Gesangbuch der Evangelischen Brüdergemein in Nord Amerika.* Bethlehem: Moravian Publication Office, 1891, p. 17, no. 47.

1963. Gombosi, Marilyn P., and McCorkle, Donald M., *The Morning Star, A Christmas Anthem for Solo and Mixed Chorus.* New York: Boosey and Hawkes, 1963. McCorkle reproduces the Moravian version of the text in his prefatory matter.

Tune of 1657

Heilige Seelenlust Oder Geistliche Hirten-Lieder, Breslau 1657, part 1, no. 26 (Zahn tune no. 1852).

Scheffler's *Heilige Seelenlust* provided melodies for its texts, seventy-five of them by Georg Joseph. This is the first tune to which "Morning Star" was set.

Subsequent Publications

1668. *Heilige Seelenlust,* 2d ed.

Tune of 1705

Geistreiches Gesang-Buch. . . , Halle, 1705 (2d ed.), no. 753 (Zahn tune no. 1853).

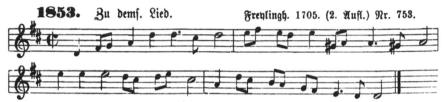

The *Geistreiches Gesang-Buch* contains 683 texts and 174 tunes with figured bass. Zahn could find no earlier source for eighty-two of the latter, although no composer is named. When the second edition was published in 1705, it contained seventeen additional new tunes, that for "Morgenstern" being among them. One of these two tunes was used as the basis for organ chorales by Kurt Doebler (b. 1896), vol. 2, and by Max Eham (b. 1915).

Subsequent Publications

1706. *Geistreiches Gesang-Buch,* 3d ed.
1719. *Geistreiches Gesang-Buch,* 11th ed.
1721. *Geistreiches Gesang-Buch,* 12th ed.
1723. *Geistreiches Gesang-Buch,* 13th ed.
1725. *Geistreiches Gesang-Buch,* 14th ed.
1727. *Geistreiches Gesang-Buch,* 15th ed.
1730. *Geistreiches Gesang-Buch,* 16th ed.
1734. *Geistreiches Gesang-Buch,* 17th ed.
1742. Johann Gottlieb Wagner, *Sammlung alter und neuer . . . Melodien,* 1742.
1746. *Geistreiches Gesang-Buch,* 18th ed.
1759. *Geistreiches Gesang-Buch,* 19th ed.
1784. Christian Gregor, *Choral-Buch,* p. 210, Art 310.

1799. Christian Gregor, *Choral-Buch*, 2d ed.
1820. Christian Gregor, *Choral-Buch*, 3d ed.
1838. Conrad Kocher, *Stimmen aus dem Reiche Gottes.*
1848. C. Karow, *Choralmelodien.*
1859. Christian Gregor, *Choral-Buch*, 4th ed.

N.B. From this date onwards, the version of the tune in common usage is simplified, all semiquavers and dots being removed.

1908. *Zpěvník evanjelické Bratrske Církve*, p. 34, no. 25.
1949. *The Moravian hymnbook with tunes authorized for use in the Moravian Church (Unitas Fratrum) in Great Britain and Ireland.* London, 1949, p. 60, no. 61.
1953. *Koraalboek der Evangelische Broedergemeente*, Zeist, 1953, p. 146, mel. 310.
1954. *Bratrsky Zpěvník*, no. 83.
1969. *Hymnal and Liturgies of the Moravian Church*, Chicago, 1969, no. 51 (no pagination).
1975. *The Moravian Liturgy with Music, Authorized for Use in the British Province of the Moravian Church (Unitas Fratrum).* London, 1975, no. 45.
1984. Christian Gregor, *Choral-Buch*, facsimile of 1st ed., Winston-Salem, N.C.: The Moravian Music Foundation Press, 1984.

Tune of 1708

Geistreiches Gesang-Buch, 4th ed., no. 752 (Zahn tune no. 1854).

In the fourth edition of his collection, Freylinghausen provided this new tune for "Morgenstern." Although he retained it for the fifth through the tenth editions, and then returned to the old tune, the new one was never published elsewhere.

Subsequent Publications

1708. *Geistreiches Gesang-Buch,* 4th ed., no. 752.
1710. *Geistreiches Gesang-Buch,* 5th ed.
1711. *Geistreiches Gesang-Buch,* 6th ed.
1713. *Geistreiches Gesang-Buch,* 7th ed.
1714. *Geistreiches Gesang-Buch,* 8th ed.
1715. *Geistreiches Gesang-Buch,* 9th ed.
1716. *Geistreiches Gesang-Buch,* 10th ed.

Tune of 1738

Harmonischer Lieder-Schatz, oder Allgemeines Evangelisches Choral-Buch, Frankfurt am Main, 1738 p. 470 (Zahn tune no. 1855).

Johann Balthasar König (late January 1691, Waltershausen near Gotha—late March 1758, Frankfurt) was a Frankfurt Kapellmeister and a productive composer. This collection was the largest produced in the eighteenth century: it contained 1,415 texts and 1,913 melodies with figured bass. By this time it was the style to smooth out rhythms, eliminating the interesting variety of earlier tunes.

Later Publications

n.d.   *Harmonischer Lieder-Schatz,* 2d ed.
1754. *Vollständiges Hessen-Hanauisches Psalmen- und Choral-Buch.*
1767. *Harmonischer Lieder-Schatz,* 3d ed.

Tune of 1744

Davidisches Harpfen- und Psalter-Spiel. . . , Stuttgart, 1744, no. 373 (Zahn tune no. 1856).

Johann Georg Stötzel (5 December 1711, Eisenach—between 1793 and 1799, Stuttgart) probably composed this setting of "Morgenstern" for this collection, which was published by Johann Georg Christian Störl. Stötzel was a cantor and teacher in Stuttgart.

Later Publications

1777. *Davidisches Harpfen- und Psalter-Spiel*, 2d ed.
1843. *Sammlung . . . Choräle und Melodien. . . .*
1855. *Zionsharfe*

Tune of 1836

Francis Florentine Hagen, "Morning Star"
  Hagen's tune for "Morning Star" must be treated with a format that is different from other tunes because there are many variants, many of them in manuscripts that appear to antedate the publications.

Sources for Hagen's "Morning Star"

Source	Date	Measures	Key	Medium	Accompaniment	Embellishment	A-section
B 885a, small score	1836?	15	B-flat	S solo, unison	entirely downward broken chords	no turn	varied
B 885a, large score	ante 1854	15	B-flat	S solo, unison	first upward broken chords, then repeated chords	no turn	varied
Bethlehem photostat	17 December 1854	15	B-flat	SA	first upward broken chords, then repeated chords	no turn	varied
L 377.1	post 1854, ante 1857	15	B-flat	S solo, SAB	harmonization only	turn not involved	varied
Beck & Lawton edition	1857	16, long 14, 15	B-flat	SATB	harmonization with repeated chords	turn	same
B 885a, organ score	post 1857?	16, long 14, 15	B-flat	instr. only	harmonization with repeated chords	turn	same
LCM Hagen	post 1857?	16, long 14, 15	B-flat		harmonization only	no turn	same
Boner edition	1890	16, long last m.	A		harmonization with repeated chords	no turn	same

Hagen's tune for "Morgenstern" consists of fifteen or sixteen measures, distributed as follows: A, four measures, repeated; B, two measures, repeated; C, three measures or four. Eight sources have turned up thus far, four of them early and four of them late.

The four early sources, one of which is dated 17 December 1854, have the following qualities: the A-section is varied when it repeats; the C-section contains only three measures (the latest version of all also returns to a three-measure C-section); and the accompaniment consists of rocking semiquavers.

Three of the late sources (one is dated 1857) have the following qualities: the A-sections are identical; in the second measure, there is a turn in the accompaniment; the C-section contains four measures; and the accompaniment consists of repeated semiquavers. The last late source, dated 1890, restores the original length (three measures) of the C-section and changes the key to A Major (all other sources, early and late, are in B-flat Major).

1836?. B 885a, small score.

The earliest copy of Hagen's "Morning Star." This is Bethlehem manuscript B 885a (small score), which may date back to 1836, when the piece was originally composed. The poor condition of the original has necessitated extensive repairs to this facsimile.

As far as I can tell, manuscript B 885a, small score (two small scraps of paper) is the earliest copy of "Morning Star." The bases for that suggestion are that it is for unison voices, it contains an accompaniment that differs from all other versions, and the hand is that of Hagen's early period (quite small; in his later years, he wrote quickly and more floridly). Indeed, this may be the original manuscript, carried by Hagen himself to Bethlehem. Hagen provides two different dates for the first performance of "Morning Star." On 23 September 1901, he remembered the occasion as follows.

Auto-Biography

> I wrote the Morning Star, a Christmas Carol, for the little school girls, with an accompaniment of stringed instruments, now 68 years ago.

The other, referring to a performance in Home Moravian Church, Salem, North Carolina, occurs in his diary of 19 December 1886, as follows:

> The Morning Star anthem was sung (too fast!!) by the choir and children, the latter seated on the south gallery. The academy girls all sat in the north gallery. The Church was crowded, as the Anthem had been specially announced several times. This is an old practice. The anthem was composed by the writer 50 years ago when teacher the Salem Boys' School for the Xmas Dialogue of the German Town girls.

Applying arithmetic to the *Auto-Biography* gives a date of 1833, when Hagen was still a student in Nazareth; doing the same to the diary gives the year 1836, when Hagen was indeed teaching at the Boys' School. The later diary date is almost certainly correct. Furthermore, since Dialogues were almost always given on Christmas Eve, the exact date of the first performance can be established as 24 December 1836, so that 24 December 1986 marks the one-hundred fiftieth anniversary of that event.

It is not as easy to settle the place of the first performance. Hagen's grandson, John Francis, wrote 27 December 1966 to Dr. Ewald V. Nolte, then director of the Moravian Music Foundation, as follows:

> "Morning Star" was first written for Sunday School children at Germanton, a short distance north of Bethania, where Grand-

father held services. However, "Morning Star" may have been sung at Bethania for the first time at a Xmas celebration.

This opinion was relayed in *Bethania in Wachovia, Bicentennial of Bethania Moravian Church, 1759–1959,* p. 77. Frances Griffin, in her article about Hagen and his Christmas piece, quotes *R,* p. 4220 (1836) to support her contention that the place was Salem.

> The girls of the town school and the Girls Boarding School gave enjoyment to various groups of the congregation with their beautifully illuminated presentations of the Christmas story and with their pleasing speeches and songs.

It seems to me that Griffin is correct, because in 1836 Hagen was not yet conducting services anywhere: he had not yet experienced his conversion; he had not been ordained; and he was not going to be associated with Bethania until 1844. Furthermore, the strings Hagen mentions were more likely to be available in Salem than in Germanton. Finally, I have found no documentation that Germanton was ever called German Town: it was Germanton on documents of 6 June 1798 (resolution to President John Adams from citizens of Stokes County, Southern Moravian Archives) and of 12 June 1811 (letter from A. D. Murphy to Frederick Meinung, Southern Moravian Archives), and it is still Germanton.

So Hagen did indeed mean that the work was first sung by the German town-girls, not by the German-Town girls (neither hyphen appears in Hagen's manuscript). Indeed, we may be able to learn from the Moravian records exactly what girls belonged to that group (they would have been enrolled in Salem Academy, and they would have been residents of Salem), and perhaps some personal diary or other document may reveal exactly who was the first Morning Star Soloist.

ante 1854. B 885a, large score.

The small and large scores are similar, but the rocking chords have been changed, and the tune is now written out in extenso. The fact that the vocal part is still in unison suggests that this copy preceded the dated copy that follows.

17 December 1854. Bethlehem negative photostat (original not discovered).

This score, exactly dated, adds an alto part to the treble as

given in the preceding manuscript. The accompaniment is the same as in that copy, but is designated "Organ." An unidentified English text, probably clipped from a periodical, was evidently pasted to the original manuscript. Here is a summary of the main differences between the two manuscripts:

> General. B 885a (large score) has only the treble part. At the end of that score is written "wird 3 mal wiederholt," but stanza 1 in German is written out in full and incipits of 2, 3, and 4 are provided. The pasted-in English translation also has four stanzas.
>
> Tempo. B 885a (large score) has *Andante;* photostat has *Slow.*
>
> m. 9. Next-to-last accompanimental semiquaver is E-flat only in B 885a (large score).
>
> m. 4. Next-to-last accompanimental semiquaver D is missing in B 885a (large score).
>
> m. 8. B 885a (large score) has  Photostat has

dynamics. All dynamics are from photostat: B 885a (large score) has none.

post 1854, ante 1857. L 377.1, untitled set of parts: S solo, SAB.

This set of parts belongs to the group of sources that includes that of 1836?, but it is later than 1836 because full SATB chorus (the tenor part is missing) was used; it is earlier than the 1857 version because the old form of the melody, with differing A-sections, was used. It is possible that this version could be earlier than 1854.

1857. *The Morning Star.*

This year marks the first published edition of Morning Star. In it, for the first time in the sources, Hagen extends the C-section to four measures by expanding the original measures 13 and 14 to create new measures 13, 14, and 15. Hagen later reverted to his original fifteen-measure form.

B 885a contains an Organo part that is identical to the printed version, except that it adds figures for the bass. We cannot know at the moment whether the manuscript or the printed version came first; however, a possibility is that the manuscript was prepared from the print to spare the organist from turning pages of the printed version. The instrumental parts in the LMC Hagen Collection go with this print.

post 1857?. B 885a, organ score.

This organ part cannot be used with the other parts that occur with it in the Bethlehem collection: it was probably made by an organist who did not want to turn the pages of the 1857 edition.

post 1857? LCM Hagen, parts.

Like the previous source, this set of parts was probably derived from the 1857 edition, but was intended for the use of a church band.

1890. *The Morning Star,* pub. W. H. Boner (see facsimile for complete cover).

New Edition Revised by the Author.

THE

MORNING STAR.

(Morgenstern.)

A Christmas Anthem,

SOLO AND CHORUS.

English Words by the

REV. MARTIN HAUSER.

Music by the

REV. F. F. HAGEN.

15 cts.

PHILADELPHIA:

PUBLISHED BY **W. H. BONER & CO.**, 1102 CHESTNUT ST.

"Morning Star," 1890 edition. Second published edition (1890) of "Morning Star." The music reprinted here is repeated exactly on two more pages, with the text of stanzas 3 and 4.

THE MORNING STAR.

English words by the Rev. M. HAUSER.

Music by the Rev. F. F. HAGEN.

SOLO.   CHORUS.   SOLO.

night. Light di - vine,   Come and shine,   Come and shine   Light di -
macht.   *Je - su - lein!*   *Komm her - ein,*   *Komm her - ein*   *Je - su -*
bright.   Je - sus Thou   Canst be - stow,   Je - sus Thou   Canst be -
weit.   *Du al - lein*   *Je - su - lein,*   *Je - su - lein*   *Du al -*

- vine   on this   dark - some heart of   mine.....................
lein   *Leucht in*   *mei - nes Her - zens*   *Schrein.....................*
- stow   more than   thou - sand suns can   do.....................
lein   *Bist was*   *tau - send Son - nen*   *sein.....................*

The Morning Star.—4.

This was Hagen's revised version, made fifty-four years after he had composed the work. In it he provides a metronome mark that interprets *Andante moderato* as 72 to the quaver. The work sounds extremely good at that speed, but every performance I have ever heard goes much faster, to the detriment of the lyric effect of the work.

The long penultimate measure in the 1857 edition fits very well with Hagen's style: he loved sustained closing passages and included them in many of his works. It may be that he first introduced the long penultimate measure in order to square off the form at a tidy sixteen measures; whatever his reason, the work is not improved here by halving the note values.

As is frequently the case in music, the original form of the work is superior to all the later ones.

1909. *The Liturgy and the Offices of Worship and Hymns of the American Province of the Unitas Fratrum or the Moravian Church,* Bethlehem, 1909, p. 305, no. 1156.

1156   Tune 310.
Morning Star, O cheering sight!
Ere Thou cam'st how dark earth's night!
  Jesus mine, in me shine;
Fill my heart with light divine.
2 Morning Star, Thy glory bright
Far excels the sun's clear light:
  Jesus be, constantly,
More than thousand suns to me.

3 Thy glad beams, Thou Morning Star,
Cheer the nations near and far;
  Thee we own, Lord alone,
Man's great Saviour, God's dear Son.

4 Morning Star, my soul's true Light,
Tarry not, dispel my night;
  Jesus mine, in me shine,
Fill my heart with light divine.
              Johann Scheffler, 1624–77.

THE MORNING STAR. [By permission.]   F. F. Hagen.

Hagen's tune was further simplified for inclusion in the 1909 Moravian Hymnal, which was the first American Moravian text-and-tune book. It should never have become a hymn. Hagen intended it as an anthem, and it belongs to a large genre of his works, namely, solo-and-chorus pieces. In addition to contravening the composer's intentions, the hymnic version necessarily eliminates the semiquaver texture that originally accompanied the lines, thus leading to the tempo increase that has become an unfortunate Moravian tradition.

Even so, the work could be better performed than it now is. The arranger (probably J. Fred Wolle) intended the organist to play the small notes in the second half of the piece, not the solo and choral parts. Even that sensitive gesture was later eliminated, because of amateur singers' imagined need always to have the organ undergirding (or obliterating) every note they sing.

The repeated editorial and executionary damage suffered by this little work underscores an artistic verity: music should be performed as the composer intended.

1920. *Hymnal and Liturgies of the Moravian Church (Unitas Fratrum),* Bethlehem, p. 41, no. 59.

1924. Winifred Kirkland, *Where the Star Still Shines.* New York: Fleming H. Revell Company, [1924], p. 7. This is a facsimile of the 1894 version.

1939. Hans T. David, *The Morning Star for Four-Part Chorus of Mixed Voices with Soprano Solo and Piano Accompaniment.* New York: G. Schirmer, Inc., 1939 (Octavo No. 8434). David's arrangement freely employs the rocking figure. He must have known the early manuscripts.

1942. Harvey Gaul, *Moravian Morning Star as Sung and Played in the Lehigh Valley on Christmas Eve by the Moravian Children* (organ solo). New York: H. W. Gray, Inc., 1942 (St. Cecelia Series no. 686). Since Gaul uses the rocking figure, his source was probably David's arrangement (1939). The work is an impressionist evocation.

1957. James Worrell Pruett, *Francis Florentine Hagen, American Moravian Musician.* Ph.D. diss., University of North Carolina, 1957, p. 111 (1857 version), p. 112 (1890 version).

1958. W. Lawrence Curry, *Morning Star. Anthem for S.A.T.B. with Youth Choir or Solo, Suitable for Advent or Christmas, Based on the Moravian Hymn by F. F. Hagen, 1815–1907.* H. W. Gray, Church Music Review no. 2566. This is an original composition that incorporates the entire simplified version of Hagen's tune, with Harvey's text.

1969. Hymnal and liturgies of the Moravian Church, Chicago, 1969, no. 51.

ca. 1974. Schmidt Musical Collectibles, Randolph, Massachusetts, item no. 291–300, is a music box that plays *Morning Star,* omitting the last phrase.

Contrafactum of 1849?

Wolfgang Amadeus Mozart, Morgenstern auf finstre Nacht, Coro . . . Ges. B. N. 79. . . . 4 stromenti & Voci in pl. & Organo/ Subj. di Mozart, L 377.2a (formerly Bethlehem 135a). This work adds the familiar "Morgenstern" text to "Laut verkünde unsre Freude" from Mozart's *Eine kleine Freimaurer-Kantate*, K. 623. The same music exists with its original text as L 377.2b; both copies came from Bethlehem.

Text of ante 1854

Translation of the German Christmas hymn, Morgenstern auf finstre Nacht. Clipping pasted to a negative photostat in the Bethlehem Moravian archives, containing Hagen's setting of the tune.

1. Morning-star! the darkness break
   Bid the world with joy awake;
      Jesus mine!
      Rise and shine:
   Fill my heart with light divine!

2. Thy transcendant brightness gleams
   Clearer than the noon-day beams;
      Such a glow,
      Jesus low!
   Not a thousand suns can show.

3. When the cheering ray we see,
   [line illegible]
      Loveliest Star,
      Near or far,
   Lord, thy worshippers we are.

4. Thee, the soul's true light, appear!
   Enter in, with haste draw near!
      Jesus mine!
      Come and shine,
   In my heart with light divine.

Text of ante 1857

The Morning Star. (Separately printed pamphlet pasted into the back cover of a copy of *The Liturgy and Hymns.* . ., Bethlehem, 1890, in the Moravian Music Foundation collections.)

1. Morning star! thy cheering light
   Can dispel the gloom of night;
      Light divine,
      Come and shine
   In this darksome heart of mine.

2. Thine effulgence, glorious light,
   Far exceeds the sun so bright;
      Jesus, thou
      Canst bestow,
   More than thousands suns can do.

3. Joyful beam, thy light we see,
   Willingly we follow thee;
      Fairest star,
      Near and far,
   Christ as God, we thee revere.

4. Therefore, oh, thou light divine,
   Come without delay and shine;
      Jesus come,
      Make thy home
   In my heart; Lord Jesus come.

The short lines reverse for the repeat in stanzas 1 and 3, but not in stanzas 2 and 4. The rhymes in stanzas 2 and 4 are faulty.

Subsequent Publications

1857. *The Morning Star ("Morgenstern in finstrer Nacht"), a Christmas anthem with solo & chorus, translated from the German by the Rev. Martin Houser [sic] of West Salem Ill., set to music and dedicated to the children of the Moravian Church by the Rev. F. F. Hagen, York, Pa. Phila. pub. by Beck & Lawton, S.E. Cor. of 7th & Chestnut. Boston: O. Ditson & Co. New York: S. T. Gordon. Cincinnati: Truax & Baldwin.* [Some words then appear in tiny type that is mostly illegible in the original and invisible in our facsimile, but which does clearly contain the date 1857.]

1883. Offices of worship and hymns, principally for use in schools, with an appendix of tunes, second and revised edition, Bethlehem, Pennsylvania, 1883, p. 16 (appendix).

1890. *New edition revised by the author, the Morning Star (Morgenstern.), a Christmas anthem, solo and chorus, English words by the Rev. Martin Hauser [sic], music by the Rev. F. F. Hagen. 15 cts. Philadelphia: Published by W. H. Boner & Co., 1102 Chestnut St., Copyright, 1890, by the Rev. F. F. Hagen.*

In stanza 1, "In" becomes "On"; in stanza 3, "revere" becomes "adore."

N. B. Rev. Daniel Jones, former pastor of Castleton Hill Moravian Church, supplied to Beatrice Schlamp a slight revision from the files of that church, made by the Rev. C. Arthur Weber, incorporating the following changes: in stanza 1, "light" becomes "sight"; in stanza 3, "Willingly" becomes "Thrillingly."

1962. Arr. James Christian Pfohl, 1962, pub. Brodt (octavo 204).

Text of 1869

Catherine Winkworth, *Christian Singers of Germany*, Philadelphia [1869], p. 250.

A Song at Day-Break

1. Morning Star in darksome night,
   Who the sad earth makest bright,
        I am Thine!
        In me shine,
   Fill me with Thy light divine!

2. Lo, Thy heaven is in me here,
   Longs to see its Star appear;
        Break of Day,
        No more delay,
   Come and chase these mists away!

3. For Thy brightness, O my Star,
   Earth's poor sun surpasseth far;
        From Thy sight,
        Lovely Light,
   Other suns must hide in night.

4. All things stand revealed by Thee,
   Past and Present and To-Be,
        And Thy smile
        Can erewhile
   Night itself of gloom beguile.

5. Where Thy joyous splendours dart
   Faith soon follows in the heart,
        Star most clear,
        Far and near
   Thou as Lord art worshipped here!

6. Come then, Golden Light of souls,
   Ere fresh darkness o'er me rolls,
        Be Thou mine,
        In me shine,
   Fill me with Thy Light divine!

Text of 1885

Bennett Hervey, *1885 Liturgy and Hymns for the Use of the Protestant Church of the United Brethren or Unitas Fratrum.* A new and revised edition. London, 1886, no. 28.

1. Morning star, O cheering sight!
   Ere thou cam'st how dark earth's night!
   >Jesus mine,
   >In me shine;
   Fill my heart with light divine.

2. Morning star, thy glory bright
   Far excels the sun's clear light:
   >Jesus be
   >Constantly,
   More than thousand suns to me.

3. Thy glad beams, thou morning star,
   Cheer the nations near and far;
   >Thou we own
   >Lord alone,
   Man's great Saviour, God's dear son.

4. Morning star, my soul's true light,
   Tarry not, dispel my night;
   >Jesus mine,
   >In me shine;
   Fill my heart with light divine.

Subsequent Publications

1911. *The Moravian Hymn Book, the Liturgy and Hymns Authorized for Use in the Moravian Church (Unitas Fratrum) in Great Britain and Ireland.* London, 1911, no. 61.
1920. *Hymnal and Liturgies of the Moravian Church (Unitas Fratrum),* Bethlehem, p. 41, no. 59.
1930. As under 1911, "revised 1912," no. 61.
1975. *The Moravian Liturgy with Music, Authorized for Use in the British Province of the Moravian Church (Unitas Fratrum),* London, 1975, no. 45.

Text of 1963

1963. *The Morning Star, by Francis F. Hagen, edited and arranged by Marilyn P. Gombosi and Donald M. McCorkle.* New York: Boosey and Hawkes, 1963 (Octavo no. 5483).

1. Morning Star, in darkest night,
   Strikes the earth with joyful light;
   > Jesulein,
   > Come be mine,
   Fill my heart with light divine.

2. Thine own sparkling splendor bright
   Far excels the sun's great light;
   > Thou alone,
   > Jesulein,
   Art a thousand suns sublime.

3. Thy luxurious radiant beams,
   Follow me eternally;
   > Fairest Star,
   > Near and far,
   Honor thee as Christ (God) the Lord.

4. Now, oh come, my soul's true Light,
   Come be mine, dispel my night,
   > Come be mine,
   > Jesulein,
   Fill my heart with light divine.

McCorkle observes,

> Fortunately, the Hauser translation was discarded by the editors
> of the *Moravian Hymnal* (1920) who used instead a version by the
> Reverend Bennett Harvey, Jr., an English Moravian minister, . . .
> It is our judgment that the Harvey version, which is quite poetic
> and traditional, is somewhat Victorian for the Classical simplicity
> of the anthem and does not accurately translate the original Ger-
> man hymn. Thus a new translation has been prepared for this
> edition which we sincerely trust will do greater justice to Fran-
> cis F. Hagen and his immensely popular anthem.

In stanza 2, one line does not rhyme; and in stanza 3, three
lines do not.

Appendix 2
Other Applications of the Term *Morning Star*

The Morning Star that ancient man knew was the planet Venus, which, because of its proximity to the sun, must be observed just before sunrise or just after sunset. It is particularly brilliant in the morning. Since its appearance in the lightening sky heralded the approach of full dawn, it was natural that the Morning Star should become a symbol of any individual who starts something, or any historical phenomenon that initiates an important sequence of events.

Thus Elinor Rice Hays titles her biography of Lucy Stone *Morning Star* because she considered her subject "a third star of equal magnitude" to the other "two great women who made and wrote suffrage history," Susan B. Anthony and Elizabeth Cady Stanton.

Similarly, *Fox's Book of Martyrs* reminds us that the "celebrated reformer . . . , John Wickliff, [was] denominated the Morning Star of the Reformation. . . . His doctrines spread into Bohemia, and were well received by . . . John Hus . . . and Jerome of Prague."

Morning Star Moravian Church in Pheonix, Arizona, began on 20 March 1977 with a meeting of twelve persons in the home of Vernon Johnson, who kindly provided information about the development of the fellowship to the status of a church on 9 October 1983. The Moravian Music Festivals, of which fifteen had taken place between 1950 and 1984, inspired the group, which occupied first a mortuary chapel, then a school, and finally a separate building.

Long before Lucy Stone, John Wickliffe, and the Arizona church, however, the Morning Star became a symbol of Jesus because he initiated man's redemption, opening the Christian era of civilization. Thus the term became a very apt one with which to christen ships that were to be devoted to spreading for the first time the light of the gospel in what the nineteenth-century missionaries considered to be the dark heathen world.

Theodore William Livingston describes these ships in "The *Morning Stars:* Ships of the 'Gospel Navy' with a Supplemental Listing of Missionary Vessels around the World," his 1971 master's thesis at the University of Hawaii at Honolulu.

Although Roman Catholic missionaries were on board ships sent out by Roman Catholic countries, the first vessel devoted exclusively to missionary work was the *Jersey Packet* of the Moravian Society for the Furtherance of the Gospel. She and her successors sailed continuously between Labrador and London from 1770 to 1926. The ships that were named *Morning Star* sailed between 1856 and 1961. They were not Moravian, and they were used chiefly in the Pacific. Livingstone provides histories and illustrations of them in his thesis.

The Moravian 1/38, 19 September 1856, p. 302, reported the proposal of the American Board of Commissioners for Foreign Missions to construct a 150-ton schooner (*The Moravian*, 1/48, 28 November 1856, called her a hermaphrodite brig) for $12,000, for the express purpose of transporting missionaries to the Micronesian islands of the Pacific. It was to be named *Morning Star,* and was to be based in the Sandwich Islands, i.e., Hawaii.

The proposal met with great success. *The Moravian*, 1/48, 28 November 1856, p. 381 reports the cost of shares in the ship as ten cents each, each share being represented by a certificate. *The Moravian*, 2/6, 6 February 1857, p. 46, reported gifts from Sabbath School children of $23,000, the price of construction rising to $13,000. The ship was built at Chelsea and launched on the Wednesday before 26 November 1856. The Moravians sent "Mr. Bingham, with his wife, son of our former Missionary Bingham, at the Sandwich Islands, to the new Mission of the Board in Micronesia."

Samuel Reinke published in *The Moravian* 2/84, 7 August 1857, p. 252, "An address to the Superintendents, teachers, and pupils of the Moravian Sunday Schools in the United States," informing us that the *Morning Star* arrived in Honolulu 24 April 1857, and quoting the *New York Observer,* 16 July 1857, as follows.

> The Morning Star was warmly received at Honolulu. The children of the Sunday-Schools and the inhabitants turned out in procession, and presented the captain, S. G. Moore, with a banner, which is about 20 feet long and 12 feet wide. The star is directly under the centre of the word "Morning." The dove is placed in the lower corner, on the right hand. The ground-work is of white bunting, and the emblems of sky-blue. A very large assembly, numbering 2 or 3,000, gathered at four o'clock, P.M., April 29th, on Market wharf and in the streets adjacent. The Morning Star was moored to the wharf, and so situated as to be in full view of the crowd. The king being absent from town, her majesty, the queen, occupied a conspicuous position upon the stairs of the market. She was attended by Prince Lot, Mr. Wyllie, and Dr. Rooke. Speeches were made by the Rev. R. Armstrong, who presented the banner, by Captain Moore, on accepting it, by Hon. John Ji, Rev. S. C. Damon, and Rev. H. Bingham, Jr. Immediately after the banner was presented, and before Captain Moore had finished his reply, the numerous audience gave cheer upon cheer, as the signal was seen floating from the masthead. Foreigners and natives, old and young, all joined in the "hurrah!"

He also quotes an anonymous letter from the Sandwich Islands.

> The Morning Star came into port on April 24th, after a very pleasant voyage of 138 days, having been detained at Rio Janeiro, eight or ten days, to have her foreyard repaired, which had been sprung in a squall. During the voyage she was visited by God's Spirit, and all her crew but one . . . , found peace with their Maker. This will surely rejoice the hearts of her thousands of owners throughout the United States. After remaining in our port one week, she sailed for the Marquesas, taking along one native missionary and his wife, besides a native chief and Rev. Mr. Emerson as delegate. After an absence of two months, she will return, and then be despatched to Micronesia. During the whole of her stay in port, she was hourly thronged by crowds of native and foreign children, each eager to secure his ten cents worth of satisfaction, (the price of a share in the vessel) by standing on the decks, and strolling through her cabins. The Morning Star will be followed by the earnest sympathies of thousands on these Islands as well as in the United States; and she will be watched and waited for here, with an interest which no other vessel afloat inspires.

Appendix 3
Musical Compositions of Francis Florentine Hagen

This list is alphabetical, but there are unavoidable inconsistencies in choices between first lines (enclosed in quotation marks) and titles (italicized). It seemed absurd to list "Morning Star" (text) under T just because its title is *The Morning Star,* and equally absurd to list *Alma mater* (title) under "O loved abode" just to be consistent in always indexing by text. So I made what I considered to be the most reasonable choice and cross referenced the alternatives.

Organ works are listed by the tune name, caps and small caps, of the hymn involved, except for some settings of hymns that are more like songs and have therefore never acquired a tune name. In those cases I simply used the text incipit. I have provided abundant cross references.

When pieces have both German and English texts, but no title, I have listed them under the text that Hagen seemed to prefer, even if some other text is better known. "Bis dereinst," for example, is familiar with the text "All the world shall sing thy praise," but I could not bring myself to accord pride of place to a text that was added later by someone else and is not a translation of the original.

I provide other information in the following order: medium; source; comments on the source; and unpublished editions and publications in chronological order.

When I first compiled this index, I followed the format of Wolfe, *Secular Music*. Since there were only fourteen prints, however, and most of them were quaint and interesting, I decided instead to print facsimiles of all of them.

"A charge to keep I have." See BOYLSTON.

1. "A friend in need is a friend indeed." Solo voice; SATB; piano. Pub. W. F. Shaw, 1883. Copy in LMC Hagen, marked "Mr. S. Peterson with compliments of the Author" and "gift of Mrs. Thomas Boyd, 1958."

"A friend in need is a friend indeed," no. 1.

2. "A loving home's a happy home." Solo voice; SATB; piano. Pub. W. F. Shaw, 1882. Cover: "Inscribed to Miss Mary E.

Johnson. . . . Words and music by Rev. F. F. Hagen." The copyright notice on the first page of music is dated 1883. Copy in LMC Hagen, marked "gift of B. J. Pfohl, 1955." Ed. Pruett, p. 140.

INSCRIBED TO
MISS MARY E. JOHNSON.

"A loving home's a happy home," no. 2.

Abend-Lied. See "Nun lege ich mich schlafen."

3. "Ach, bleib' mit deiner Gnade" ("Jesus, all-creating Word"). SAB; organ. LMC Hagen ms.: two sheets marked "Organo. Brr. Gsbch. 951." Ed. Pruett, p. 110.

4. ADESTE FIDELES. Organ solo. *OC* II, p. 81. Hagen calls the work a "Voluntary."

"All hail the power." See CORONATION.

"All the world shall sing his praise." See "Bis dereinst mein Stündlein schlägt."

5. *Alma mater.* Solo voice; SATB; piano. Pub. Lee & Walker, 186 Chestnut Street, Philadelphia, Pennsylvania, 1854. (See illustration in Chapter 2.) The cover also bears a picture of the old structure, drawn by A. Fray and engraved by T. Sinclair. Text incipit: "O loved abode!" Four copies in LMC Hagen: one inscribed "Found at New Dorp 1960, gift of the Hagen heirs

1961"; one framed. Ed. Pruett, p. 136.

"Am I a soldier of the Cross." Organ solo. See ARLINGTON.

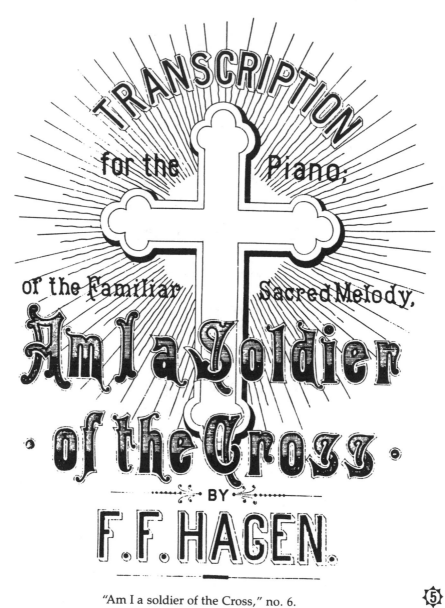

"Am I a soldier of the Cross," no. 6.

6. "Am I a soldier of the Cross." Piano solo. Pub. W. F. Shaw, 1882. Copy in LMC Hagen, inscribed "gift of Mrs. Thomas Boyd 1958."

7. "And I heard a voice from heaven" (solo) and "Blessed are the dead" (chorus). Solo S; SATB; organ. B 930, called "Requiem" on cover. New Dorp I, p. 24, called "Requiem" in title. Art 22A is quoted, marked at the end to be sung by the congregation. This is one of a set of four pieces, three of them dated, whose grouping in Bethlehem suggests that it is probably the second work composed in August 1878 (see comment on no. 54, "Praise waiteth . . .").

8. "And the seventh angel" (T recitative) and "The kingdom of this world" (chorus). New Dorp III, p. 25. Title: "Doxology in the Apocalypse. Rev. XI.15.16.17. . . . Jan 1880."

9. ANTIOCH. Organ solo. *OC* II, p. 2.

10. ARLINGTON. Organ solo. *OC* I, p. 46.

    ARLINGTON. Piano solo. See "Am I a soldier of the Cross." Piano solo.

11. "As the bark floateth on." Voice; piano. Pub. John Cole, Baltimore, n.d. (plate no. 1000). Title: ". . . Song of Glaucus, from the Last days of Pompeii." The name L. W. Webb is printed at the end of the text. Electrostatic copy in LMC Hagen, original not discovered. The work is listed in the Firth & Hall catalogue (1870).

    "Awake, and sing the song." See BOYLSTON.

12. BALERMA. Organ solo. *OC* II, p. 58. Text: "The Lord is my shepherd."

    "Before Jehovah's glorious throne." See OLD HUNDREDTH.

13. BETHANY. Organ solo. *OC* I, p. 84. Ed. Boeringer, pub. Brodt, 1985.

14. "Bis dereinst mein Stündlein schlägt" ("Till at last mine hour shall come"). SATB; strings; organ. B 753, with instrumental parts. Rau & David, p. 115, says that this copy was made by Till, who died in 1844. New Dorp III, p. 12, titled "Chorus (Funeral service) Till at last mine hour shall come. . . ."; p. 13, "Words translated from the German by Rev. L. F. Kampmann." S 404; also listed as 214b in the Salem alphabetical catalogue, but missing. Ed. David, 1939, pub. New York Public Library, *Music of the Moravians in America*, no. 12. Ed. Dickinson, 1954, with the text "All the world shall sing thy praise," pub. Gray MCM 10. Ed. Pruett, p. 90.

    "Blessed are the dead." See "And I heard a voice from heaven."

    "Blessed Saviour, thee I love." See SPANISH HYMN.

    "Blow ye the trumpet." See LENOX.

15. BOYLSTON. Organ solo. *OC* II, p. 26. Text: "A charge to keep I have" or "Awake and sing the song." Ed. Boeringer, pub. Brodt, 1985.

16. BRATTLE STREET. Organ solo. *OC* II, p. 77. Text: "While thee I seek, protecting power."

    "By cool Siloam's shady rill." See SILOAM.

17. CANAAN. Organ solo. *OC* II, p. 68. Text: "Oh! that will be joyful."

    Cantata. See "Herr, wie sind deine Werke so gross." See *Christmas Cantata.*

    "Children of the heavenly father." See PLEYEL'S HYMN.

18. *Christmas Bells* ("Hark, the Christmas bells are ringing"). Voice; piano. Pub. W. F. Shaw, 1882. Cover: ". . . A beautiful old English song." Copy in LMC Hagen, inscribed "gift of Mrs. Thomas Boyd 1958."

Christmas Bells, no. 18.

19. *Christmas Cantata.* SATB; strings; flute; 2 cornets; trombone. Instrumental parts dated 1891 are in the possession of Mrs. Elizabeth Pfaff, and a photostat of these is in LMC Hagen. The text and choral parts are missing, but the original sections and incipits can be derived as follows from the parts.

Part I. Prophecy. 1.˙Introduction; 2. Tenor solo "Lovely Eden" (2 verses), Chorus "O Eden! Eden!"; 3. Quintett "Lost Eden" and "Eden, lovely Eden" (2 verses); 4. Chorus "Fare thee well"; 5. Chorus "Sin hath cursed thee"; 6. Chorus "A glorious King"; 7. Recitation; 8. Quartett and Chorus "Will he come?"; 9. Recitation; 10. Chant "Praise the Lord"; 11. Recitation and Response (3 girls); 12. Chorus "The Redeemer will come"; 13. "Come, Saviour, come"; 14. Recitation; 15. Duet "We have longed."

Part II. Advent. 16. Alto solo "Coming, yes, coming"; 17. Recitation; 18. Chant "Praise the Lord," Intermezzo; 19. Chorus with tenor solo "The Redeemer is come"; 20. Tenor solo "Tell it o'er the . . ."; 21. Chorus "Sing it out"; 22. Bass solo; 23. Recitation; 24. "Glory to God"; 25. Soprano solo "Chiming bells are pealing"; 26. Recitation; 27. *The Lily Song;* 28. Chorus and Quartett "Let us worship," "With the angels rejoicing"; 29. Final chorus "Crown him."

John Franklin McCuiston, in his "Diary for 1891, January 1st to . . . April 30th 1892" (Southern Moravian Archives) records that he "kept the Elm St. Meeting" every Saturday night (this establishment was a Sunday school, and the expression "Elm St. Meeting" appears on Hagen's parts). Occasionally Bishop Rondthaler presided. On Saturday evening, 26 December 1891, McCuiston records that he "attended . . . the Elm St. S. S. exercises in the Home Church." His remark almost certainly refers to the performance of Hagen's cantata.

Church and Home organist's Companion, a Choice Selection of Voluntaries, Consisting of Anthems, Reveries, Transcriptions of Well-Known Hymn Tunes, Prayers, Marches, etc., etc., etc., Arranged for the Pipe or Reed Organ, by Rev. F. F. Hagen.

This large collection appeared as eight periodical numbers, four each year in September, December, March, and June, between September 1880 and June 1882. Each issue contained twenty-four pages, and these were later gathered into two hardboard volumes of ninety-six pages each, plus front matter. The foundation holds one complete hardbound specimen given by the Hagen heirs, one imperfect hardbound copy, and three specimens of the periodical issues (vol. I, nos. 1 and 2, and vol. II, no. 1), one of which was given in 1982 by Robert Whiting, who also provided an eight-page advertising brochure.

The most important segment of *OC* is the set of thirty-nine organ preludes composed by Hagen. They are listed in Chap-

ter 6. The rest of the collection consists of ninety-two arrangements of music by thirty-three other composers. The
composers are named, and the number of works by each is
provided, also in Chapter 6.

It is possible that more works are involved than those
tabulated in the previous paragraph, because the two hardbound sets in the foundation collections do not match each
other, the periodical specimens, or the indexes that Williams
printed at the ends of the volumes. Pieces are moved around,
new works are substituted, and one large chunk of one hardbound copy appears to come from a completely different
collection that was produced in the same format. Oddly, all
the pagination is in proper sequence: perhaps one of Williams's workers could decipher only numbers.

Christmas Carol. See "Hail, thou wondrous infant Stranger."
See "What good news the angels bring."

"Come, O Creator Spirit blest." See FEDERAL STREET.

"Come, thou fount of every blessing." See NETTLETON.

"Come, ye disconsolate." See CONSOLATOR.

"Come, ye that love the Lord." See ST. THOMAS.

20. CONSOLATOR. Organ solo. *OC* I, p. 6.

21. CORONATION. Organ solo. *OC* I, p. 12. Text: "All hail the
power of Jesus' name."

22. CROSS AND CROWN. Organ solo. *OC* II, p. 84. Text: "Must
Jesus bear the Cross alone."

"Dem Lamm der gepflanzt ist." See "Unto the Lamb that was
slain."

Dirge. See "Songs of praise the angels sang."

Doxology. See "Unto the Lamb that was slain."

Doxology in the Apocalypse. See "And the seventh angel
sounded."

23. DUKE STREET. Organ solo. *OC* II, p. 37. Text: "Jesus shall reign
where'er the sun" or "O happy day that stays my choice."

"Fear not, for behold, I bring good tidings." See "Siehe, ich
verkündige euch grosse Freude."

24. FEDERAL STREET. Organ solo. *OC* I, p. 80. Text: "Come, O
Creator Spirit blest."

25. "Florentine" Waltz. Lost work mentioned by John Francis
Hagen in a letter of 27 December 1966.

"From every stormy wind that blows." See RETREAT.

"From Greenland's icy mountains." See MISSIONARY.
Funeral. See "Bis dereinst mein Stündlein schlägt." See
"Lord, let thy blest angelic bands."

"Gentle river, the moonbeam is hush'd." See *The Lay of the
Troubadour.*

26. "God is our refuge." SATB; 2 flutes; 2 clarinets; bass trombone; organ. Source not discovered. Ed. Pruett, p. 1.

"God is the refuge of his saints." See WARD.
HAGEN. See "Morning Star."

27. "Hail, thou wondrous infant Stranger." SAB; keyboard (colla parte). New Dorp II, p. 24. Title: "Christmas carol for three voices." LMC Hagen. S 461.2 (two S parts only).

"Hark, the Christmas bells are ringing." See *Christmas Bells*.

28. "Her last words at parting." Voice; piano. LMC Hagen, manuscript, inscribed "given by Mrs. Thomas Boyd 1958."

29. "Herr, wie sind deine Werke so gross und viel." SATB; strings; 2 flutes; 2 clarini in C; 2 clarinets in C; 2 horns in C; bassoon; bass trombone; organ. B 346. B 75.4. This copy was made by Till in 1840 for $2.25. The second page bears the entire text, after which the instrumentation is listed, concluding "Comp. di Fr. Hagen, Professor in Nazareth Hall." Ed. B. J. Pfohl. Ed. Pruett, p. 12. Rau & David observes, p. 115,

> This . . . is by far the most extended sacred composition written by an American Moravian. . . . [It] is amateurish in various respects, but includes many excellent details. The first movement and the end of the last, for full chorus, are well sustained and harmonically interesting. The second movement is fugal, with continuous modulation. The third movement is attributed to single voices, evidently soli. The character of the composition makes it probable that it was one of Hagen's early attempts at composing, and that it was written before Hagen came to the Northern Province for the second time.

The authors also reproduce the first page, plate W. David mentions the work with similar enthusiasm in his preface to his edition of "Bis dereinst."

30. "Home, sweet home." Organ solo. OC II, p. 71 (periodical format, II, p. 95).

31. "How amiable are thy tabernacles." S solo; SATB; strings; flute solo, ad lib. B 929. At the end: "Bethlehem Pa. Aug. 31. 1878." Above the score: "Ps. 84, 1.2."

32. HURSLEY. Organ solo. OC I, p. 26. Text: "Sun of my soul, thou Saviour dear."

33. I'M A PILGRIM. Organ solo. OC II, p. 32. The tune is an "anonymous Italian air." Text: "I'm a pilgrim."

I'm a Pilgrim, no. 34.

34. *I'm a Pilgrim.* Piano solo. Title: "Transcription for the piano of the beautiful sacred melody, I'm a pilgrim." Pub. W. F. Shaw, 1882. Copy in LMC Hagen, inscribed "gift of Mrs. Thomas Boyd 1958."

"Immanuel" Cantate. See *Christmas Cantata.*

"In the Christian's home in glory." See Rest for the Weary.

Invocation. See "Kyrie eleison." See "Praise waiteth for thee."

"It is finished." See Zion.

"Jesu, du, o Herze ohne gleichen." See "O delightful theme."

"Jesus, all-creating Word." See "Ach, bleib' mit deiner Gnade."

"Jesus, lover of my soul." See Martyn.

"Jesus shall reign." See Duke Street.

"Joy to the world." See Antioch.

35. "Kyrie eleison" ("Saviour, have mercy"). SATB; organ. Listed (S 96.4) in the Salem alphabetical catalogue, but missing there. New Dorp I, p. 1. Title: *Invocation.*

36. Laban. Organ solo. OC I, p. 66. Text: "My soul, be on thy guard." Ed. Boeringer, pub. Brodt, 1985.

37. Lenox. Organ solo. OC II, p. 46. Text: "Blow ye the trumpet, blow."

38. "Lift up your heads, O ye gates." SATB; strings; flute; 2 clarinets in B-flat; 2 clarinets in C; 2 horns in B-flat; 2 horns in E-flat; trombone; contrabass; organ. LMC Hagen. Vocal and instrumental parts inscribed "given to the Foundation 26 August 1982 by Mrs. Margaret Weidner." Wrapper inscription: "Lift up your heads, O ye gates (Hagen) for Palm Sunday, from Miss Amy Van Vleck, Salem, N. C." LMC Hagen, multiple copies made by B. J. Pfohl; multiple copies made in 1924 and 1928 by J. L. Kapp for Calvary Moravian Church, Winston-Salem, North Carolina. S 250.4, listed in the alphabetical Salem catalogue, but missing. S 406.1. Arr. James Christian Pfohl, 1945, pub. Brodt 101. Ed. Pruett, p. 38.

39. "Lob, Preis und Dank." SATB. Title: "Tisch-Lied auf dem Essem zu singen. Die Worte und die Musik von F. F. Hagen." With a work dated "Nov. 1898" ("Nun lege ich mich schlafen"), given to the foundation by Raymond S. Haupert (letter, 13 December 1965). These are probably Hagen's last compositions.

40. "Lobsinget Gott" ("Sing praise to God"). SATB; strings; 2 flutes; 2 clarinets in B-flat; 2 horns in E-flat; trombone; organ. New Dorp II, p. 1. Notation: "Ascension." S 408, subtitled on the organ part, "Zu Himelfahrt [*sic*]." Listed in the Salem alphabetical catalogue at 213.3, but missing.

41. "Lord, let thy blest angelic bands." SATB; organ. S 407.2, 409, subtitled "Funeral." Ed. Pruett, p. 109.

42. MARTYN. Organ solo. *OC* I, p. 39. Text: "Jesus, lover of my soul."

43. MISSIONARY. Organ solo. *OC* I, p. 31. Ed. Boeringer, pub. Brodt, 1985.

   "Morgenstern." See "Morning Star," Appendix 1.

44. "Morning Star." See Appendix 1.

45. "Mowing the harvest hay." Voice; SATB; piano. Text by Minnie Gilmore. Dedication: "To Mrs. Mary Johnson Woodhead" (see also "A loving home's a happy home"). Pub. W. F. Shaw, 1887. Copy in LMC Hagen.

"Mowing the harvest hay," no. 45.

"My days are gliding swiftly by." See SHINING SHORE.

"My soul, be on thy guard." See LABAN.

"Nearer, my God, to thee." See BETHANY.

46. NETTLETON. Organ solo. *OC* I, p. 18. Text: "Come, thou fount of every blessing."

47. No SORROW THERE. Organ solo. *OC* I, p. 62. Text: "O sing to me of Heaven."

48. "Nun lege ich mich schlafen." SATB; piano (colla parte). Title: *Abend-Lied.* LMC Hagen, found by Raymond S. Haupert among his father's papers, and given to the foundation 1965 (see his letter, 13 December 1965). Dated "Nov. 1898." See also "Lob, Preis und Dank."

"O come, all ye faithful." See ADESTE FIDELES.

"O delightful theme," no. 49. New Dorp holograph.

49. "O delightful theme" ("Jesu, du, o Herze ohne gleichen").
    SATB; organ. New Dorp II, p. 1, dated "Feb. 5, 1836." Listed
    as S 292.1b in Salem alphabetical catalogue, but missing. Ha-
    gen heard this work performed Saturday, 9 April 1887, at
    New Philadelphia Moravian Church, more than fifty years
    after he composed it. Ed. Boeringer, in *A Moravian Anthem
    Book*, pub. Brodt, 1984, p. 23.

    "O happy day, that stays my choice." See DUKE STREET.

    "O loved abode." See *Alma mater.*

    "Oh, sing to me of heaven." See NO SORROW THERE.

    "Oh! that will be joyful." See CANAAN.

50. OLD HUNDREDTH. Organ solo. *OC* II, 25 (periodical format:
    II, p. 98). Text: "Before Jehovah's glorious throne."

    "Onward, Christian soldiers." See ST. GERTRUDE.

51. Overture in F Major. PSB 1366.12. Cover: "Overture com-
    posed and respectfully dedicated to the Members of the Or-
    chestra at Bethlehem P^{a}. by F. F. Hagen." Edited for the
    Fleisher Collection of the Free Library of Philadelphia.

52. PLEYEL'S HYMN. Organ solo. Text: "Children of the heavenly
    King."

53. "Praise waiteth for thee." S solo; SATB; organ. B 931, titled
    Invocation and dated "Aug. 1, 1878." Ed. Pruett, p. 113.

    Hagen records in his diary, 19 August 1878, that he had
    been sick for six weeks with typhoid fever and spinal neural-
    gia, and "wrote a good deal, amongst the rest two original
    choruses." This work must be one of the two, and the other
    may be "And I heard" (no. 7). Hagen evidently continued
    composing past the date of the diary entry, for "How ami-
    able" (no. 31) is dated 31 August 1878.

    Psalm 82. See "How amiable are thy tabernacles."

54. "Remembrance" Rondoletto. Cover: ". . . dedicated to his
    friend Wm. B. Binninger Esqr. by F. F. Hagen. Pub. J. L.
    Hewitt & E. I. Jaques, 239 Broadway. Two copies in LMC
    Hagen, one original without cover, one electrostatic with
    cover. A mid-nineteenth-century manuscript copy, probably
    of the printed edition, survives in the Salem Music Books
    Collection 21.4. Certainly this work was composed and pub-
    lished before Bininger's death in 1841, and it might well have
    come out while he and Hagen were still in Nazareth together,
    i.e., ca. 1839. This dating is approximately verified by Vir-
    ginia Larkin Redway's *Music Directory of Early New York City*,
    which establishes that the Hewitt & Jaques imprint was used
    only between 1837 and 1841.

from F. F. H

REMEMBRANCE

Rondoletto

For the

Piano Forte

COMPOSED & DEDICATED

TO HIS FRIEND

Wm G. F. Finninger Esq.

By

F. T. HAGEN.

Pr.50c

NEW·YORK

Published by J. L. Hewitt & E. J. Jaques 239 Broadway.

"Remembrance" Rondoletto, no. 54.

Requiem. See "And I heard a voice from heaven."

55. REST FOR THE WEARY. Organ solo. *OC* I, p. 56. Text: "In the Christian's home in glory" (Hagen uses the chorus, "There is rest for the weary," as his title).

56. RETREAT. Organ solo. *OC* II, p. 34. Text: "From every stormy wind that blows."

Rienzi. See *The Lay of the Troubadour.*

"Rock of ages, cleft for me." See TOPLADY.

Rondoletto. See "Remembrance" Rondoletto.

57. ST. GERTRUDE. Organ solo. *OC* I, p. 74. Text: "Onward, Christian soldiers."

58. ST. THOMAS. Organ solo. *OC* II, p. 20. Text: "Come, ye that love the Lord."

"Saviour, breathe an evening blessing." See VESPER HYMN.

"Saviour, have mercy." See "Kyrie eleison."

59. *Scherzo capriccioso.* Piano solo. LMC Hagen, formerly SCPL unnumbered. Title: ". . . composed & very respectfully dedicated to Rev. C. A. Van Vleck by F. F. Hagen." Stamp: "Received under the will of Miss A. Van Vleck, August 1929." Ed. Pruett, p. 142.

60. "Schlaf, liebes Kind." SATB; strings; organ. B 755.1, dated 1834. L 344.2. This copy was made by Till in April 1835 for $1.12. The work is the first of *Zwei Stücke* (see also "Sel'ge Lebensstunden"). Ed. Pruett, p. 117.

61. "Sel'ge Lebensstunden." SATB; strings; organ. B 755.1, dated 1834. L 344.2. This copy was made by Till in April 1835 for $1.12. The work is the second of *Zwei Stücke* (see also "Schlaf, liebes Kind").

62. SHINING SHORE. *OC* I, p. 89.

63. "Siehe, ich verkündige euch grosse Freude." S solo; SATB; strings; 2 flutes; 2 clarinets in C; 2 horns in D; trombone; organ. S 407.1. Ed. Pruett, p. 63 (a separate edition by Pruett is also in LMC Hagen). Ed. Gombosi, 1963, pub. BH 5482 with the text "Fear not, for behold I bring good tidings." First modern performance 19 June 1964, Seventh Moravian Music Festival, Bethlehem, Pennsylvania, and 14 October 1973, Friedberg Music Festival, Winston-Salem, North Carolina.

64. SILOAM. Organ solo. *OC* II, p. 16. Tune: "By cool Siloam's shady rill."

"Sing praise to God." See "Lobsinget Gott."

Song of Glaucus. See "As the bark floateth on."

65. "Songs of praise the angels sang." SATB. New Dorp II, p. 34. Hagen published this work as an organ solo in *OC* II, p. 41, oddly titled *Dirge.*

66. SPANISH HYMN (Hagen's tune name: SPANISH CHANT). Organ solo. *OC* II, p. 89. Text: "Blessed Saviour, thee I love."
"Sun of my soul." See HURSLEY.

67. "The earth is the Lord's." SATB? LMC Hagen, soprano part only. This is a doubtful work, identified as being Hagen's only by a notation on the envelope containing it.

68. *The Grave of My Wife* ("With snow all bedight"). Voice, piano. Pub. G. Andre and Co., 1104 Chestnut Street, Philadelphia, 1866. The text is by Rev. W. C. Reichel, under whose name the work is listed in the Firth & Hall Catalogue. Copy in LMC Hagen, signed "M. J. Reichel."

The Grave of my Wife, no. 68.

69. THE GREAT PHYSICIAN. Organ solo. *OC* II, p. 50. Text: "The great physician now is near."

"The kingdom of this world." See "And the seventh angel."

The Last Days of Pompeii. See "As the bark floateth on."

70. "The last rose of summer." Organ solo. *OC* II, p. 54.

71. *The Lay of the Troubador.* Voice, piano. Subtitle: "from Rienzi by E. L. Bulwer." Text by "G. W. Quidor, Esqr." Text incipit: "Gentle river, the moonbeam is hush'd on thy tide." Pub. James L. Hewitt, 239 Broadway. Electrostatic copy in LMC Hagen, original not discovered. Virginia Larkin Redway, *Music Directory of Early New York City*, p. 41, establishes that Hewitt was at 239 Broadway from 1836 to 1843, thus providing the latest date for the composition of the work.

"The Lord is my shepherd." See BALERMA.

The Mercy Seat. See WARD.

"The morning light is breaking." See WEBB.

The Morning Star. See "Morning Star," Appendix 1.

"There is rest for the weary." See REST FOR THE WEARY.

72. "There'll be no more sorrow there." Piano solo. Pub. W. F. Shaw, 1882. Copy in LMC Hagen, inscribed "gift of Mrs. Thomas Boyd 1958."

"Till at last mine hour." See "Bis dereinst mein Stündlein schlägt."

73. TOPLADY. Organ solo. *OC* I, p. 2. Text: "Rock of ages, cleft for me."

74. "Unto the Lamb that was slain" ("Dem Lamm der gepflanzt ist"). SATB; organ. B 927, inscribed "Bethlehem Pa̱ June 12, 1879." New Dorp II, p. 25. Ed. Pruett, p. 125 (text not included).

75. VESPER HYMN. Organ solo. *OC* II, p. 64. Text: "Saviour, breathe an evening blessing."

76. WARD. Organ solo. *OC* II, p. 74. Text: "God is the refuge of his saints." Ed. Boeringer, pub. Brodt, 1985.

77. WATCHMAN. Organ solo. *OC* I, p. 50. Text: "Watchman, tell us of the night." Ed. Boeringer, pub. Brodt, 1985.

"Watchman, tell us of the night." See WATCHMAN.

78. WEBB. Organ solo. *OC* I, p. 94. Text: "The morning light is breaking."

79. "What good news the angels bring." SATB (another version, SATB-SATB); organ. New Dorp II, p. 13. LMC Hagen, two copies given 26 August 1982 by Mrs. Margaret Weidner. Title: ". . . 61, Christmas-tide Antiphonary. Dedicated to the Rev. J. Taylor Hamilton, Pastor of the Second Moravian Church,

Transcription

FOR
THE
PIANO

OF THE

BEAUTIFUL SACRED MELODY

There'll Be no more Sorrow There.

by

F. F. HAGEN.

⟨5⟩

"There'll be no more sorrow there," no. 72.

The Token, piano solo.

Philadelphia. . . ." The voices are SATB and "juvenile." S 461.2, S part only. Ed. McCorkle, n.d., from the New Dorp copy, inscribed "first modern performance, First Moravian Church, Bethlehem, Centennial, December 1962." Since J. Taylor Hamilton was Pastor of Second Moravian Church 1881–1886, the latest possible data of composition can be inferred.

"While thee I seek." See BRATTLE STREET.

"With snow all bedight." See *The Grave of my Wife.*

80. "Ye are come unto Mount Zion." S solo; SATB; strings; flute; organ. B 928, dated 1879. New Dorp I, p. 8. S 389, dated October 1853.

81. ZION. Organ solo. *OC* II, p. 61. Text; "It is finished."

Zwei Stücke. See "Schlaf', liebes Kind" and "Sel'ge Lebensstunden."

Additional

The Token. Piano solo. Pub. Kretschmar & Nunns, N°. 70 S°. Third & & 196 Chesnut [*sic*] St^s, Philadelphia, Pennsylvania, n.d. The only known copy of this work was given by Mrs. Margaret Turner in 1983 as part of the Siewers Collection, too late to be included in the list. No *Fine* is indicated, and it is possible that the work continues to a second sheet that is missing.

Appendix 4
Biographies

Biographies are provided here for the following categories of individuals.

Hagen's brothers and sisters. They included Louise Cynthia, Ernest Julius, Augusta Maria, and Johanetta Florentina.

Hagen's children. He had, as it were, two families. He and his first wife Clara Cornelia Reichel had six children: (1) Clara Amelia, (2) Susan Frederika, (3) John Cornelius, (4) Francis Benjamin, (5) Miriam, and (6) Felix Florentine. He and his second wife Ellen Smyser had five more children: (7) William Timoleon, (8) Beatus, (9) Ernest Smyser, (10) Harry Rice, and (11) Samuel.

Other musicians named Hagen. Many other musicians bore the name Hagen (Hagan, Hagius, van Hagen, von Hagen) without being necessarily related to Francis Florentine, whose genealogy at this time goes back only to his father, Johann Joachim. This appendix provides biographical matter and lists of works, all under the surname Hagen. At the end of these entries is a list of unlocated musical works that I know only from attributions to an unqualified "Hagen" in secondary sources. These individuals are Amand van der; Friedrich Heinrich von der; Gottlieb Frederic; Gregor; Hieronymus; J. B.; Joachim Bernhard; Peter Albertus [?] van, Jr.; Peter [Albrecht]? van, Sr.; Sebastian; Sophus Albert Emil; and Theodor. I solicit further information.

Hagen's publishers. These were G. André, James M. Beck (& Lawton), William Henry Boner, John Cole, James Lang Hewitt, Lee & Walker, William F. Shaw, and Frederick Williams.

André, G.

G. André (no biographical details discovered) published music in Philadelphia from 1851 to 1879 (when bought by Ditson) at 19 S. 9th Street and at 1104 and, later, 1228 Chestnut Street (Gerson, p. 367). He brought out Hagen's *The Grave of My Wife* (no. 68) in 1866.

Beck, James M.

The individuals involved in the partnership of Beck & Lawton, which lasted only from 1856 to 1863, were James M. Beck and Dennis Lawton (no biographical details discovered). There were many persons named Beck among the Moravians, but no connection has been discovered. The firm brought out the first edition of Hagen's "Morning Star" (no. 44; see Appendix 1) in 1857.

Bininger, William Burger

Hagen dedicated his "Remembrance" Rondoletto to William Burger Bininger (4 November 1818, New York City—17 [Schwarze says 2] May 1841, Rome Italy). Many members of this family attended Nazareth Hall. William Burger entered in 1830, about the same time as Hagen, and graduated from Moravian College in 1839, a member of the ninth class. Sources: New Dorp, New York, gravestone; Schwarze, *History of the Moravian College*; ms. "Church Register Begun in the year of our Lord 1801," pp. 53, 180.

Böhler, Petrus, alias Peter

Petrus Böhler (31 December 1712, Frankfurt on Main—27 April 1775, London) became a preacher with Spangenberg in England and America. Source: [Theodor Erxleben], *Das Hilfsbuch für Liturgen und Organisten in den Brüdergemein*, Gnadau, 1891.

Boner, William Henry

William Henry Boner (20 April 1840, Winston-Salem, North Carolina—18 December 1913, Philadelphia, Pennsylvania, published the second edition of Hagen's "Morning Star" (no. 44; see Appendix 1) in 1890. He was, according to the *Bulletin* of the First Moravian Church of Philadelphia, 13/3, January 1914, p. liv,

> in his earlier years an active worker in the First Church, a member of the trombone choir, and an ever-ready helper with his gifts in singing or organ-playing.

Boner's parents were Joshua and Elizabeth Crist Boner, and he was twice married, to Clarissa L. Freeman and to Mary C. Hoats. Gerson, p. 370, informs us that W. H. Boner and Co. was a Philadelphia music publisher at 1102, 1314, and 1419 Chestnut St., Philadelphia, from 1865 to 1900. Boner was organist of Calvary Presbyterian Church from about 1870 to 1880. He brought out music by Moravian and other composers, publishing the second edition of Hagen's "Morning Star" (no. 44; see Appendix 1).

Cole, John

John Cole (c1774, Tewkesbury, England—17 August 1855, Baltimore, Maryland), according to Samuel Pease Cheney, *The American Singing Book*, 1870, p. 186, came to America in 1785 and eventually established himself as a bandmaster, compiler, teacher, and composer. He published Hagen's "As the bark floateth on" (no. 11) at an unknown date.

Freylinghausen, Johann Anastasius

Johann Anastasius Freylinghausen (2 December 1670, Gandersheim, Brunswick—12 February 1739, Halle) is the possible composer of the 1705 tune for "Morning Star." He was the devout and highly capable pastor of Saint Ulrich's Church in Halle. In addition to his successful pastoral work, Freylinghausen also ranks, according to Mearns, "not only as the best of the Pietistic school, but as the first among his contemporaries."

Hagen, Amand van der

Amand van der Hagen (no known relationship; c1753, Antwerp—July 1822, Paris) was a clarinetist, composer, and arranger. *RISM* lists four concertos, ten sets of six duos each, and numerous arrangements, by Amand Jean François Vanderhagen. The foundation has (SCM 307) *Six Walzer Six Allemandes pour Flut et Violon composé par A van der Hagen prix f 12 No 150 chez N. Barth a Rotterdam.* A vendor's label has been mostly scraped away, leaving "... ported ... Sold ... ₵ 18 ... Ma ... S ...." This might be Wolfe, no. 9456, unlocated.

Hagen, Augusta Maria

Augusta Maria Hagen (16 April 1824, Salem, North Carolina—2 February 1895, Salem, North Carolina), was Hagen's second child. She remained in the town of her birth all her life, teaching in the Girls Boarding School. The Helfer Conferenz reports her being hired 28 October 1842 (*R*, p. 5087). There is another note of hiring 13 February 1845 (*R*, p. 5139). One of her diaries is in the Old Salem, Inc., collections, and her Memoir is in the Southern Moravian Archives. Hagen notes that when he returned to Salem 5 March 1886, he "saw my sister Augusta."

Hagen, Beatus

Beatus (Latin: *blessed*) was Hagen's eighth child, stillborn in 1866.

Hagen, Clara Amelia

Clara Amelia (not Clara Cornelia as listed by Pruett; 3 August 1842, Nazareth, Pennsylvania—date and place of death unknown) was Hagen's first child.

Auto-Biography

But it pleased the Lord to deepen this good work by a ... experience, in the death by croup of our first born child, Clara Amelia, who sleeps in Nazareth Cemetery.

My inordinate grief over the death agonies of my child presently showed me that I loved that child more than I did Christ. I now prayed for more love to Christ, & that I might weep over the sufferings of Christ as much, yea, far more, intensely than ever before. And to this day the remembrance of the bleeding form of Jesus moves my heart's affections more than anything else can do.

Memoir

From then on I needed all my inner strength to face many severe tests, especially the home-going of our beloved only child, Clara.

Oh! how painful it was, especially when death at last came, that I still did not love my Saviour and my God more than all else, and that I truly loved my child more than the Saviour who had been crucified for me, and that I counted his death for naught.

However, through this and full many other troubles I sought opportunities to discover and to savor even in my spiritual poverty, the eternal loving grace of God.

Hagen, Ernest Julius

Ernest Julius Hagen (places and dates of birth and death unknown) was Hagen's brother, the second child born to his parents. No further information has been discovered.

Hagen, Ernest Smyser

Ernest Smyser Hagen (1 May 1868, New Dorp, Staten Island, New York—24 April 1956, place not identified) was Hagen's ninth child and evidently his favorite son, for it was Ernest who was to carry on his father's ministerial and evangelical work. He was also a musician, playing violin. Hagen tells us in his diary (20 July 1886):

> Ernest & Harry played in the orchestra who assisted the Chatauqua entertainments . . . by playing violin & eating cake & ice cream.

Programs in the MMF collections tell that on 23 May 1908, he played a sextet by Klassert, and on 28 November of the same year he was a first violinist in a concert present by the Orchestral School, directed by Paul E. Beck in New Linden Hall Auditorium, playing three works by Pleyel (Op. 8, nos. 1, 2, and 5) and an assortment of other music.

Ernest was salutatorian of his Seminary class. Much information about him is contained in a scrapbook that he received 25 December 1889, such as clippings describing his marriage (27 June 1889) to Louisa (Loula) Copper (1869–1937) and his ordination and installation at Edgewater Moravian Church, Staten Island. He also served First Moravian, Philadelphia; Lebanon; York; and Lititz. While in the two last-named pastorates, Hagen lived with him, coming to know many of his grandchildren.

Ernest also was President of the P.E.C. North and President of the Board of Trustees of Moravian College and Theological Seminary. That institution awarded him an honorary doctorate 8 June 1927. When Ernest's son J. Francis Hagen was salutatorian at Nazareth Hall Commencement exercises 13 June 1906, he represented the third generation to graduate from the institution.

The scrapbook also describes the wedding of Ellen Elizabeth Hagen and Fred Wilson Pfaff in the Old Chapel, Heckewelder Place, Bethlehem. Ernest, her father, conducted the ceremony; she was given by her brother, Ernest S. Hagen, Jr.; and his sister, Mrs. Oscar E. Mills, of New Dorp, was matron of honor. Mr. and Mrs. Pfaff inspired the present book and supported its writing spiritually and financially.

The Hagen and Pfaff families encountered each other many years ago, for F. F. Hagen baptized Francis Wesley Pfaff, Fred's grandfather, on 14 November 1845 in Bethania. I am grateful to the Rev. William A. Cranford and Archivist Mary Creech for documentation (Bethania Church Book) of this coincidence.

Hagen, Felix Florentine, Jr.

Felix Florentine Hagen, Jr. (3 October 1855, place unidentified—place and date of death unknown) was Hagen's sixth child.

Hagen, Francis Benjamin "Ben"

Ben Hagen (3 March 1848, place unidentified—date and place of death not discovered) was Hagen's fourth child, and seems to have continued his involvement in his father's later life more than did the other children of Hagen's first marriage.

Hagen had financial and domestic difficulties in his later years, moving from place to place with confusing and pathetic frequency. In 1882, for example, after leaving his Philadelphia position, he writes that he "returned as a dernier resort to my dear son F. Benjamin, a resident at the time in Tremont, New York. I spent a week with him from Tues. 27 June to July 3ᵈ."

Less than a month later (1 August 1882) he had return to Ben, "sick & sad at heart." He remained about two weeks and then secured private lodgings in that neighborhood. He left Tremont 10 October 1882.

There is no doubt that his time in Tremont was a low point in his life. On 5 September 1882, he reported, "Today I am here 6 weeks, paid up board by carpet, $20. Board $3 a week, have credits of $2 on next week." The next day he wrote a

> letter to Brn. Schultze & Schweinitz asking for an appointment. Surely goodness & mercy shall follow me all the days of my life. And I will dwell in the house of the Lord forever. Ps. 23:6. Tho' dark be my way, yet since he is my guide, 'Tis mine to obey, & 'tis his to provide. Though cisterns be broken, And creatures all fail, The Word he hath spoken Will surely prevail. Amen! & Amen!

Ben apparently left the church entirely, and his doing so deeply saddened his father. On 8 December 1886, however, Hagen jubilantly reports in his Salem diary "Had . . . a paper from Ben, Tremont, . . . which caused me unspeakable joy. Ben and Ida have resumed their former church relations (in the Tremont M. E. Church). God has again vouchsafed to help them."

His joy continued the next day (9 December 1886): "Pray on, my soul, pray ever. . . . Bright moments sometimes come to me, in spite of my deserts."

Hagen, Friedrich Heinrich von der

Friedrich Heinrich von der Hagen (19 February 1780, Schmiederburg—11 June 1856, Berlin) was a writer on musical subjects, not connected, so far as is known, with Hagen.

Hagen, Gottlieb Frederic

Gottlieb Frederic Hagen (fl. 1721), unconnected, so far as is known, with Hagen, published, according to Fétis, vol. 4, p. 198, a musical study.

Hagen, Gregor

Gregor Hagen (fl. 1576), not known to be connected with Hagen, is mentioned by Eitner as a tenorist at the Dresden court chapel.

Hagen, Harry Rice

Harry Rice Hagen (10 May 1870, place not known—date and place of death unknown) was Hagen's tenth child, probably named after William Henry Rice. Harry Rice was a boarding student at Nazareth Hall and visited his father in Philadelphia during the Christmas holidays, 21 December 1882–9 January 1883. The boy was musical, at least to the extent that Hagen was able to record (20 January 1887), "Harry bought a good E-flat trombone cornet à piston, made by Lamotte, Paris."

Hagen, Hieronymous

Hieronymous Hagen (fl. 1666), not connected with Hagen, is mentioned by Eitner as a Braunschweig musician.

Hagen, J. B.

J. B. Hagen (fl. 1845), no connection to Hagen known, is mentioned by Fétis, vol. 4, p. 198, as a music director in Bremen who composed songs with piano accompaniment and published in Hamburg and Hanover some music for four male voices.

Hagen, Joachim Bernhard

Joachim Bernhard Hagen (fl. 1759–1766), no known connection with Hagen, is mentioned by Eitner as a chamber musician and lutenist in Bayreuth c1766. The Augsburg city library has a 1759 manuscript containing lute works by him.

Hagen, John Cornelius

John Cornelius (6 September 1846, unknown place—date and place of death unknown), was Hagen's third child and first son. I have found no further information.

Hagen, Louise Cynthia

Louise Cynthia Hagen (26 October 1817, Salem, North Carolina–19 December 1884, Salem, North Carolina) was Hagen's sister and oldest sibling. Their father, Johann Joachim, asked the Aufseher Collegium 22 August 1836 (*R,* p. 4227) "whether a certain Mr. Sussdorf, who tuned a small organ in the Girls Boarding School, might tune the organ in the church." The response was negative. A year after that, 4 September 1829 (*R,* p. 4276), Johann Joachim reported to the Aufseher Collegium that "he has boarded a certain Mr. Sussdorf, who is going to stay in his house from time to time."

In that same year Louise Cynthia married Br. Christian Friedrich Sussdorf (*Memorabilia* 1839, *R,* p. 4454). We can be sure that

Christian Friedrich was the same as the organ-tuning Sussdorf because Hagen reported 11 October 1844 (*R*, p. 4804), while he was minister at Bethania, "My dear brother-in-law Sussdorf has been with us today and tomorrow will repair our organ."

Minnie J. Smith (*R*, p. 4276, footnote) concluded that this was the same person as a Mr. Sussdorf

> who brought the first stereopticon lantern, or magic lantern, to Salem and . . . gave exhibitions in the Salem Tavern. . . . In later years he decided to move west, loaded his goods in a wagon, and with his family started on his way. He travelled about two miles, halted, liked the looks of the place, unloaded his goods and settled there, where he built his home and remained to the end of his days.

I should surmise, however, the stereopticon Sussdorf was John William, who was married to Catherine Elizabeth (Sliferd) Sussdorf. It was one of their eight children, Christian Friedrich (Frederick) (28 August 1807, Eisenach, Germany–15 July 1886, Salem, North Carolina), who tuned the organ, stayed with Johann Joachim, became a Moravian, and married Louise Cynthia. It would be interesting to know where young Sussdorf gained his knowledge of pipe organs.

In his diary, 15 July 1886, Hagen records that

> In the evening there was, about 10 o'clock, a very heavy thunderstorm & an uncommonly sharp clap of thunder. About this time the soul of C. F. Sussdorff took its flight into eternity. He died of cancer of nearly two years' standing. His face and neck were eaten away, & not being able to assimilate what little food he could take in a soft or liquid form, he finally died of exhaustion, being nearly 79 years of age. He had been my sister Louisa's husband till last December a year ago, when she died. Strange that this man's death should be the first record made in this diary.

One of the children of that marriage was Hagen's nephew Frank, whom he mentions in his personal diary (18 March 1883) as then living at 506 Pine Street, "a poor penitent, returned to the Lord's table after an absence of many years." Hagen visited him 6 and 7 April 1883 "in order hear of his mother, my sister, who is reported very sick at Salem, N.C."

Hagen, Miriam

Miriam Hagen (10 January 1853, place not identified—date

and place of death not discovered) was Hagen's fifth child. I have discovered no other information.

Hagen, Johannette Florentina

Johannette Florentina (no information about birth and death) was Hagen's sister, the fourth child of Johann Joachim.

Hagen, Peter Albertus[?] van, Jr.

Peter A. van Hagen, Jr. (c1780, Charleston, South Carolina– 12 September 1837, New York?), no connection with Hagen, was, according to Richard J. Wolfe, in *Secular Music*, p. 333, the son of Peter Albrecht? and Catherine Elizabeth van Hagen, adding that the father and son nevertheless called themselves Peter A., Sr. and Jr. *Baker's* lists them both as Albrecht, and *RISM* lists three works for Peter Albrecht von Hagen with no qualification.

Wolfe tells us that the younger van Hagen was "first mentioned in New York concert programs in 1789 as a pianist 'eight years of age'": hence the estimate of 1780 as the year of his birth; when he died, his age was noted as 58. He began to teach in 1792 and in 1796 moved with his family to Boston, where he became a publisher, composer, teacher, organist, and violist.

His works include the following. Songs, all but "To arms . . ." (n.d.) dated 1802. *Anna; Gentle Zephyr; Kiss the Brim and Bid It Pass; May Morning; The Pride of Our Plains; To Arms, Columbia; Will Not Dare to Tell.* Piano soli. *Governor Eustis's March; Governor Eustis's Quickstep.* He also arranged a work by Briljan, *President Munroe's Trumpet March;* and *Baker's* lists an overture.

Hagen, Peter [Albrecht]? van Hagen, Sr.

Peter A. van Hagen, Sr. (1750, Holland [Eitner says Hamburg]—date and place of death unknown) was, according to Burney, vol. 3, p. 250, an organist in Rotterdam in 1772. In 1774 he emigrated to Charleston, South Carolina, where he became a music teacher. He spent from 1789 to 1796 in New York City and then moved to Boston. In addition to "much theatre music," *Grove's* lists *Federal Overture* (1797), *Funeral Dirge on the Death of George Washington* [1800], and a song, *Adams and Washington,* as works by him.

Hagen, Samuel

Samuel Hagen (no information about dates and places of birth and death) is not listed in the Hagen birthday book, but only in diary references. On the occasion of Hagen's sixty-fourth birthday (30 October 1879), he mentions receiving letters from five children, among them "Sam[1],", and on 24 June 1883, Hagen notes that "Samuel came from Iowa." On his sixty-seventh birthday (30 October 1882) Hagen notes that he had "letters from Sam[1]. my son & others." And on 23 August 1885, that he "returned to Iowa not being able to find work here. I supplied him with $28.00 for traveling & other expenses, but it was with a heavy heart that I saw him leave & have ever since been filled with forebodings of evil." On 28 August 1883, Hagen "had a card from Sam. dated 26th Iowa City. He now repents having returned west & wishes he had stayed here. If he is sick & sad, I am equally so. He wrote the day after his arrival on Sunday & is disappointed in not finding work. . . . I wish he had not gone."

On 30 October 1883, however, Hagen wrote, "Today I am 68 years old. God rejoiced my heart in causing me to receive, by his overruling lovingkindness, a letter from my son Sam in Iowa, on whose account I had suffered great anguish of mind, not knowing what had become of him after he left me last August. He seems well."

8 April 1885. "Samuel arrived from the West in a sad plight & was taken to Nazareth on the next day."

Hagen, Sebastian

Sebastian Hagen (fl. 1595–1604), no connection with Hagen, is mentioned by Eitner as an organist in Zabern.

Hagen, Sophus Albert Emil

Sophus Albert Emil Hagen (3 May 1842, Copenhagen–3 April 1929, Helsingor), no connection with Hagen, was chiefly an editor, researcher, and writer in the field of music.

Hagen, Susan Frederika

Susan Frederika (25 May 1844, unknown place—date and place of death unknown) was Hagen's second child. On 28 December 1879 he received a letter from her in Bethlehem. At that time she was married to a man named Gosling and was living in Crittenden, Kentucky. On 10 February 1887, he mentioned another letter from her, this time from Ravenswood, Virginia, "after a long silence. Answered her and sent her a book soon after."

Hagen Theodor

Theodor Hagen (15 April 1823, Hamburg [Fétis says Dessau]–21 December 1871, New York City), unconnected with Hagen, so far as we know, was a composer of many published songs and piano pieces. Most of the citations at the end of these Hagen entries probably refer to works by him. Fétis, vol. 4, p. 198, mentions three nocturnes, Op. 3, that were published in Hamburg.

Hagen, William Timoleon

William Timoleon Hagen (25 March 1865 [the last digit is unclear in the Hagen birthday book], Bethlehem, Pennsylvania—date and place of death unknown) was Hagen's seventh child. He was living in Philadelphia at 1421 Vine Street during Hagen's unwilling and unhappy sojourn in Tremont, New York. That they remained close is demonstrated when, on 10 October 1882, Hagen records, "took up my abode with my son Willie, 1421 Vine Street" who was then only seventeen, but evidently already living on his own. A week later (17 October 1882) Hagen suffered a stroke, but by 29 October was able to go out again. Hagen remained with Willie until 12 May 1883, when he moved to Mrs. Revear's (?) house at 330 Franklin Street. Willie is frequently mentioned in the diaries as paying a visit, sending a letter, or otherwise demonstrating filial concern.

Unidentified "Hagen" Attributions

The *Firth and Hall General Catalogue* lists two works by Francis Florentine Hagen (*The Grave of My Wife* and the "Remembrance" Rondoletto); a song, *Lady of England*, attributed to "Hagen"; and a *Bethlehem Waltz* and *Lancaster Waltz* attributed to "Hagan".

The *Board of Music Trade Catalogue* lists two works by Francis Florentine Hagen ("As the bark floateth on" and "Morning star"), as well as the following pieces attributed to "Hagen": a *Christmas Anthem; Cradle Song; Faribol* (which is listed under the general category of "Rondos, fantasias, variations, &c."); *Gail-*

larde (Morceau de genre); Impromptu; Reverie; and *Little Galop.*

The Moravian Music Foundation solicits copies of any of these works.

Harvey, Bennet

Bennet Harvey (4 January 1829, Gracefield, Derry, Ireland–24 November 1894, Ockbrook, England) was the son of Bennet and Deborah Wheater (Blackburn) Harvey. He was educated at Fulneck, Niesky, and Gnadenfeld and served the Moravian church (minister unless otherwise noted) at Fulneck (master), 1851–1858; Kilwarlin, 1858–1864; Westwood (Home Mission), 1864; Kingswood, 1865; Wyke (minister and director of the Girls' School), 1865–1868; Malmesbury, 1868–1873; Bath, 1873–1876; Dublin, 1876–1883 (also principal from 1879); and Ockbrook (also director of Girls Boarding School), 1884–1894. He was a member of the Committees for the Revision of the Hymnbook 1878–1885, and contributed one original text and a number of translations, among them a translation of "Morning Star." Source: J. N. Libbey, *The Moravian College, 1860–1910, Fairfield, near Manchester,* n.p., 1910, p. 21, supplied by Henry Williams, Moravian College, Bethlehem, Pennsylvania.

Hauser, Martin

Martin Hauser (23 September 1799, near Salem, North Carolina–25 October 1875, Hope, Indiana) was the translator of the ante 1857 text of "Morning Star." He experienced a conversion at a revival in 1827, and in September 1829 he moved to the Indiana wilderness, where he founded Hope. There he functioned as "exhorter and liturgus" until he was ordained Deacon 10 March 1833 in Bethlehem, whereupon he became minister in the town he had founded, remaining until 1847.

He then became minister at West Salem, functioning as a home missionary in the area. With Tietze he organized Enon (1845), and with Senseman he organized Olney (31 July 1853). From 1853 to 1861 he was the English minister at West Salem (there were then two Moravian congregations, one English and one German). He retired to Olney, then moved to West Salem, and finally he returned to Hope, where he died. (Source: Edmund de Schweinitz, "The Clergy. . . ." manuscript in the northern archives, kindly searched by Robert Steelman.)

In the newly initiated *Moravian,* 1/13, 28 March 1856, p. 98, John H. Eberman informs us that Martin Houser supervised the signing of a Brotherly Agreement 25 May 1844 in West

Salem, Illinois, and preached the following day (Whitsunday) in a barn. Houser became the called Pastor in 1847, being replaced 31 December 1851 by Edwin T. Senseman, who was in turn replaced, December 1855, by Eberman. The Moravian Publication Office published Hagen's *In Memoriam* on Senseman, who died 8 February 1866 at Hope, Indiana. Eberman continues:

> Our church is quite a neat building, but rather small. Instead of a steeple, we have a sort of "gallows-looking affair," a few yards from the church, on the top of which hangs a large good-toned bell, lately presented to the church. Formerly a dinner-horn announced meeting-time! Inside of the church there is a choir gallery. Without boasting, we have a good choir here, and, what is least expected, a first rate trombone choir. The present church chandelier is one of the five used lately in the Bethlehem church. We have no organ, but we are at the moment trying to procure a melodeon.

Hauser began many congregations in the Midwest. In the *Moravian*, 1/10, 7 March 1856, p. 73, he supplied a letter (25 January 1856) describing an independent congregation there, unaffiliated with any denomination, which called pastors as it chose. A number of the independents, mostly English from the southern part of Edwards County, visited West Salem for an anniversary service 27 May 1849. They asked Hauser to preach to them, and he began to do so once a month. Work progressed until Hauser finally, after much soul-searching, permitted them to sign a Brotherly Agreement, thus establishing at Albion a new Moravian Home Mission congregation.

Hauser first visited Olney 16 September 1851. He was asked to preach and did so in the courthouse and in the open air, because there was no church building at all in the town. Things went well, however, and a building was consecrated 17 September 1854.

Hauser contributed regularly to the *Moravian*, such as 1/30, 25 July 1856, when he digressed on the imminent severance of the American Synod from Herrnhut, and on church tunes.

> Church tunes and ritual have a far greater bearing on the Church than we may suppose. The idea that uniformity is not essential to unity is, in my opinion, incorrect. Church tunes are considered non-essential. . . . Those . . . who take this view . . . can never have given it their serious consideration. . . . Singing is that part of worship in which all can take a part, and according to the participation will be the enjoyment. No part of worship addresses itself more to the passions than singing. . . . I have seen

brethren from Germany completely overpowered by the sound
of the organ, melodeon, or trombones, or a familiar tune sung by
the congregation. They at once felt themselves at home.

Therefore Hauser believed that the German tunes had to be
preserved, and to do so, he suggested that

every minister should consider it part of his duties to teach singing; and thereby also arouse the slumbering patriotism of our
church.

Hauser and Hagen evidently had a good relationship.
Hauser wrote regularly to the *Moravian* while Hagen was an
editor, and Hagen spent his last active years serving in Hauser's area of the Midwest. Hagen mentions other members of
the family in his diary, such as 21 August 1886, when he and
Ernest were taken by "George Hauser, from the neighborhood
of Hobbs' (Dobbs'?) Chapel . . . to his house (the old Benjamin
Hauser place), where we remained over night," apparently so
that Hagen could preach early the next day at a Methodist
revival.

Hewitt, James Lang

James Lang Hewitt (1807–1853) was the son of the composer
and publisher James Hewitt. He continued his father's business
after the older man died in 1827, and had premises at 239
Broadway from 1836 to 1843, with Jaques as partner from 1839
to 1841; hence the datings assigned these works by Hagen that
he published: "Remembrance" Rondoletto (no. 54), ante 1841;
and *The Lay of the Troubadour* (no. 71), ante 1843.

Joseph, Georg

Georg Joseph (fl. 1657) was the composer of the earliest
known tune for "Morning Star." Zahn's biography no. 105
identifies him as a musician or music director in the Breslau
Fürstbischoff chapel. Elsewhere (tune no. 1852) Zahn praises
the "rich inventiveness" of Joseph's tunes, noting that they are
like arias and employ bright and varied rhythms.

Reichel, William Cornelius

William Cornelius Reichel (9 May 1824, Salem, North
Carolina—25 October 1876, Bethlehem, Pennsylvania), Ha-

gen's first father-in-law, wrote the words for Hagen's song *The Grave of My Wife* (no. 68). He was the son of Gotthold Benjamin Reichel, principal of Salem Female Academy. He became a teacher at Nazareth Hall in 1844, later teaching at Bethlehem Moravian schools. In 1858 he became a professor in the Theological Seminary, in 1862 principal of Linden Hall, and in 1870 professor at the Bethlehem Seminary for Young Ladies. Source: *Moravian* 21, 2 November 1876, p. 176 (obituary). The names of seven members of the Reichel family appear in the Hagen birthday book.

Rice, William Henry

William Henry Rice (8 September 1840, unidentified place—date and place of death not discovered) was Hagen's faithful friend, whom he made guardian of his three youngest children. Harry Rice Hagen may have been named for him.

Hagen was one of five preachers at the dedication of the new church at York, Pennsylvania, 25 October 1868, about five months after Rice had taken over (30 May 1868). Rice remained there until 1876 and then moved to Nazareth. Hagen reported (12 May 1879), "Nazareth is in great commotion over Br. Rice's removal by the P.E.C." He then apparently went to First Moravian, for Hagen comments (15 October 1882) as follows.

> Attended 1st Moravian Church in the morning. Br. Rice preached a very strong sermon on "To every man his work." He made a very lucid and cogent statement of his views on the present crisis of the Moravian Church. Very humiliating, it is true, but very salutary, if heeded by the parties concerned. Its application not only belonged to 1st Church, but to the American Province in general.

Rondthaler, Ambrose

Ambrose Rondthaler (8 June 1813, York, Pennsylvania–7 September 1890, Bethlehem, Pennsylvania) first taught at Nazareth Hall 1832–1835. He was ordained Deacon 23 April 1837 and became assistant minister at Gnadenhutten, Ohio, 1837–1839 He was minister at Graceham 1839–1844, Camden Valley 1844–1846, Emmaus 1846–1853, and York 1853–1854, immediately before Hagen. Then he served as principal in Bethlehem 1857–1871, retiring to open his own school there, but returning to the Moravian school to teach in 1883. Source: Hacker, *Bethlehem*.

Scheffler, Johannes

The original German text of "Morning Star" is by Johannes Scheffler, alias Angelus Silesius (1624, Breslau, Silesia–9 July 1677, Breslau, Silesia). The author was a Lutheran physician who so involved himself in Roman Catholic mysticism that he eventually became a Franciscan monk. His *Heilige Seelenlust* is his most significant work. It was published in four volumes in 1657, a fifth being added in a second edition in 1668. The musical settings were composed or supplied by Georg Joseph.

Although Scheffler was a Roman Catholic when he produced the book, his hymns became quite popular with the Lutherans and even more popular with the Moravians. Zinzendorf included 79 of his texts in his *Christ-Catholisches Singe- und Bet-Büchlein* of 1727. In Mearns's opinion,

> unfortunately, precisely the worst were selected for imitation, so that Scheffler has the doubtful honor of being the model of the spiritual-fleshly productions which disfigured the Moravian hymn-books between 1740 and 1755.

Schweinitz, Robert William de

Robert William de Schweinitz (20 November 1819, Salem, North Carolina–20 October 1901) was educated at Nazareth Hall and at Moravian College and Theological Seminary. He taught at Nazareth Hall 1839–1845 (Hagen was there until 1841) and then went to Europe, where he married (1846). He returned to teach at the Theological Seminary and to be pastor at Graceham (1849) and Lancaster (1849–1853). Then he began his tenure at Salem Female Academy, remaining there through the Civil War. In 1866 he became principal of Nazareth Hall. He was also president of the P.E.C. in 1878 and 1887. Source: Dorothea de Schweinitz, *Summary History*, p. 22ff.

Schweinitz, Edmund Alexander de

Edmund de Schweinitz (20 March 1825, Bethlehem, Pennsylvania–18 December 1887) was, with Hagen and Kampmann, the third founding editor of the *Moravian*.

Schweinitz, Emil A. de

Emil A. de Schweinitz (16 October 1815, Salem, North Carolina–3 November 1879) was, Hagen observed in his diary, "a fellow student, fellow teacher, & fellow minister of mine ever since 1828. I have outlived him one year."

Senseman, Edwin Timoleon

Edwin Timoleon Senseman (18 December 1818, Salem, North Carolina–8 February 1866, Hope, indiana) was Hagen's contemporary. Hagen preached a memorial sermon 18 March 1866 at New Dorp, Staten Island, New York, which was later published. It seems likely that Hagen named his son in honor of Edwin Timoleon Senseman.

Shaw, William F.

William F. Shaw (information about birth and death not discovered) was, according to Gerson, p. 408,

> one of the first publishers to sell cheap sheet and bound music. Folios in book form sold for about fifty cents a copy on news stands, sheet music five cents and up.

He was an active worker in Second Moravian Church, Philadelphia. He founded Fifth Moravian Church in 1877 and was licensed to preach. He was ordained in 1878 and became pastor there, resigning in 1879 because of ill health. In 1880 he became pastor of Fourth Moravian Church in Philadelphia, with Hagan as his assistant. Shaw resigned in 1882 (Hagen with him), again on account of ill health. He then turned back to secular work. Most of the Hagen music that he published came out while the two were working together at Fourth Moravian Church.

Shaw kept up his interest in the church, however, and established yet another one, the first service at which is described (7 January 1888) as follows by Hagen, who had moved to Philadelphia 6 June 1887, settling at 614 Diamond 26 September 1887:

> Snow & rain & storm. Ernest & I accompanied Br. [illegible initials] Blum to the new church, to be called Grace Mor. Church (Br. W. F. Shaw's gift to the Morav. Church) in order to start a Sunday School. We found about 13 people there, half a doz. children & the rest adults. In the School room, Br. Blum opened by singing & then called on me to pray & then he read the S. S. lesson & discoursed on it, whereupon he asked me to make some additional remarks, which I did. Ernest offered up the closing prayer & I accompanied the Doxology, L.M. on the organ & thus that

place of worship was opened. The dedication of the church by a Bishop! will be postponed until the deed for the church is in the hands of the P.E.C. The rain penetrated the roof [illegible words] & the platform is thoroughly soaked in many places & will probably drop off & cause an expense of hundreds of dollars to repair. The church is gaudy enough, but not well constructed. It is moreover quite out of the way & hard to find, while the new Baptist church is on the Germantown Av., a public thoroughfare. The public shool, however, is kept in the anterooms of the church, bringing in a rental of $700 a year, out of which Br. Blum & myself are to be paid. At this writing I know of *no one* who will join! & it is an interesting question to me, if a church shall ever be gathered here.

In 1882 Shaw published "Am I a soldier of the Cross" (no. 6), *Christmas Bells* (no. 18), "I'm a pilgrim" (no. 34), and "There'll be no more sorrow there" (no. 72); in 1883, "A friend in need is a friend indeed" (no. 1) and "A loving home's a happy home" (no. 2); and in 1887 "Mowing the harvest hay" (no. 45).

Silesius, Angelus: see under Scheffler, Johannes.

Sussdorf: see under Hagen, Louise Cynthia.

Van Vleck, Amelia "Miss Amy" Adelaide

Amelia "Miss Amy" Adelaide Van Vleck (18 October 1835, Lancaster, Pennsylvania–1929, Winston-Salem, North Carolina) was, according to Jane Van Vleck, *Ancestry and Descendents of Tielman Van Vleck of Niew Amsterdam*, 1955, p. 294, connected with Salem College, teaching piano, guitar, and mandolin. She was a good musician, even though Hagen observed in his diary,

> 18 January 1887: "My first appearance as Philharmonic leader. Had more trouble to keep the accompanist (Amy V.V.) from playing out of time than in drilling the entire chorus." 22 January: "The Philharmonic accompanist has struck for a salary! $ per month, Miss A.V.V. threatening to resign if refused! If she knew how to keep time, her services might be worth something." 8 February: "The accompanist A.V.V. got nervous and ever recalcitrant when corrected. Conceited amateurs are troublesome at times."

Van Vleck, Charles Anthony, alias Carl Anton

Charles Anthony Van Vleck (4 November 1794, Bethlehem,

Pennsylvania–21 December 1845, Greenville, Tennessee) taught at Nazareth Hall 1813–1823. He was ordained Deacon 6 July 1823, and served as a minister in Bethania 1823–1826, Newport 1826–1834, Lancaster 1834, York 1835, and Nazareth 1836–1839. During this last pastorate, he was also simultaneously principal of Nazareth Hall. Subsequently he became professor in the Theological Seminary at Bethlehem 1839–1844. He left there to become principal in Tennessee, where he died. Source: Hacker, *Nazareth*. He was an active composer and published many songs. He and Hagen were together in Nazareth 1837–1839, and *Scherzo capriccioso* (No. 59) probably originated during that time.

Van Vleck, Henry J.

Henry J. Van Vleck (biographical details not discovered) was an Ohio Moravian pastor and composer to whom Hagen appealed when he found himself jobless and homeless in 1877.

Van Vleck, Jacob

Jakob Van Vleck (24 March 1751, New York City–3 July 1831, Bethlehem, Pennsylvania) was educated at Barby, served in various capacities in various American Moravian centers, and became Bishop in 1815. He left only a few compositions; nevertheless, according to Rau & David, p. 53, they show that he was a fine musician.

Van Vleck, Lisetta Maria

Lisetta Maria Van Vleck (13 April 1830, Newport, Rhode Island–19 September 1914, Winston-Salem, North Carolina) left a number of piano works that are now in the foundation collections.

Van Vleck, Louisa "Miss Lou" Cornelia

Louisa "Miss Lou" Cornelia Van Vleck (20 August 1826, Bethania, North Carolina—22 April 1902, Winston-Salem, N. Carolina) was also a musician who taught at Salem College.

Van Vleck, William Henry

William Henry Van Vleck (14 November 1790, Bethlehem, Pennsylvania–January 1853, Bethlehem, Pennsylvania) was one of the three members of the first class of the Moravian Theological Seminary, then in Nazareth, Pennsylvania. He was consecrated a Bishop 20 November 1836, and ordained Hagen as a Deacon 19 September 1844. He held many positions in the following locations: Nazareth 1809; Bethlehem 1816; Philadelphia 1817; Nazareth 1822; New York 1836; Salem 1836; Bethlehem 1849.

Unidentified "Van Vleck" attributions

Most of the music of these various members of the Van Vleck family has not been catalogued, and it has not been possible to locate copies of even their published works, so that most of the following "Van Vleck" attributions from nineteenth-century catalogues cannot yet be assigned to particular individuals.

Board of Music Trade Catalogue. Songs: 1. *Early Friends*; 2. *The Hope, the Star, the Voice*; 3. *On Prayer*; 4. *Star of Evening*. Waltzes; 5. *Blue-eyed Susette*; 6. *Happy Childhood*; 7. *Memories of the Past*. Galops; 8. *Nettie*. Marches and Quicksteps; 9. *Carolina*. Four hands: 10. *Brignal Banks*.

Firth & Hall Catalogue. Songs: 11. *Glorious Things of Thee Are Spoken*; 12. *High Let Us Dwell in Tuneful Notes*.

Williams, Frederick

Frederick Williams (no biographical details discovered) published Hagen's *Home and Church Organist's Companion* between 1880 and 1882.

Winkworth, Catherine

Catherine Winkworth (13 September 1829, London–July 1878, Monnetier, Savoy) was a gifted translator of German texts into apt and elegant English. She produced two major collections of texts (*Lyra Germanica*, first series, 1855; second series, 1858); one collection of texts and tunes (*The Chorale Book for England*, 1863); and one biographical study (above). There she provides a biography of Scheffler and translates two of his texts "from those less commonly quoted," one of them being a lovely version of "Morgenstern" that, so far as I know, was never set to music and never republished until now (see Appendix 1, Text of 1869).

Woosley, Samuel Augustus

Samuel Augustus Woosley (10 May 1846, near Friedberg, North Carolina–8 September 1898, Friedberg, North Carolina) educated himself and became a licentiate of the Moravian Church, serving Friedland, New Philadelphia, Providence, Oak Grove, and Macedonia. Hagen observed (19 August 1886),

> I know but two men in this province who have unction & energy enough to lead the army of the Lord, which is comparatively idle in our country churches . . . , & these are Brethren Rights & Woosley. The latter, though he is licensed to labor in the Word and doctrine, which he does with much power & with great acceptance, is not yet episcopally fitted out with the right of wearing a surplice, marrying people, & administering the sacraments. Paul, however, thought it of infinitely greater importance to convert souls to God than to baptize men with water.

Abbreviations

Aelt. Confz.	Aeltesten Conferenz (Council of Elders)
B	Bethlehem Congregation Collection
Br.	Brother
Brn.	Brethren
L	Lititz Congregation Collection (see Bibliography, s.v. Steelman)
LMC	Later Moravian Composers Collection
M.E.	Methodist Episcopal
MMF	Moravian Music Foundation
OC	*The Home and Church Organist's Companion*
P.E.C.	Provincial Elders' Conference
PSB	Philharmonic Society of Bethlehem Collection
pub.	published by
R	*Records of the Moravians in North Carolina*
S	Salem Congregation Collection (see Bibliography, s.v. Cumnock)
SCPL	Salem College Permanent Loan Collection
Sr.	Sister
T	*Transactions of the Moravian Historical Society*

Bibliography

Albright, S. C. *The Story of the Moravian Congregation at York, Pennsylvania.* York [1927], p. 167f., portrait opp. p. 168.

Baker's Biographical Dictionary of Musicians. 5th ed. Revised by Nicholas Slonimsky, with 1971 supplement. New York, 1971, s.v. Hagen.

Board of Music Trade of the United States of America Complete Catalogue of Sheet Music and Musical Works. 1870. Facsimile ed. New York, 1973, s.v. Hagen.

Boeringer, James. "Francis Florentine Hagen (Moravian Composers Series, part II)." In *Journal of Church Music* 24, no. 8 (October 1982): 2.

Cumnock, Frances. *Catalog of the Salem Congregation Collection.* Chapel Hill, 1980, 96.4, "Kyrie eleison," no. 35; 213.3, 408, "Lobsinget Gott," no. 40; 214.4, 404, "Bis dereinst," no. 14; 250.4, 406.1, "Lift up your heads," no. 38; 292.16, "O delightful theme," no. 49; 316.3, 452, "Morning Star," no. 44; 389, "Ye are come," no. 80; 407.1, "Siehe, ich verkündige," no. 63; 407.2, 409, "Lord, let thy blest angelic bands," no. 41; 461.1, "Hail, thou wondrous infant Stranger," no. 27; 461.2, "What good news," no. 79.

David, Hans T. "Musical Life in the Pennsylvania Settlements of the Unitas Fratrum." In *Transactions of the Moravian Historical Society* 13 (1942): 19, reprinted as MMF Publication (monograph) no. 6, 1959.

Eitner, Robert. *Biographisches-bibliographisches Quellen-Lexikon . . . ,* Leipzig, 1901, s.v. Hagen.

Fétis, F. J. *Biographie universelle des musiciens,* Paris, 1873, s.v. Hagen.

Firth & Hall. *General Catalogue of Fashionable and Popular Music, Published and for Sale by Firth & Hall, No. 1, Franklin Square, New York.* n.d.

Griffin, Frances. "The Man Who Wrote 'The Morning Star,' " In *Moravian Music Foundation Bulletin* 24, no. 2 (Fall–Winter 1979): 11.

Hacker, H. H. *Nazareth Hall, an Historical Sketch and Roster of Principals, Teachers, and Pupils.* Bethlehem, 1910.

Hagen, Francis Florentine. Hagen's Auto-Biography. This document survives in two holograph forms. "Auto-Biography Written at the Request of a Dear Christian Friend at York Pa September 23 1901." Ms. in the Moravian Archives, Bethlehem, Pa.; copy in the MMF Research File, s.v. Hagen. "Auto-Biography written at the request of a Christian friend, York, Pa." Ms. in the Moravian Archives, Bethlehem, Pa.; copy in the MMF Research File, s.v. Hagen.

————. Birthday book. See Reichel, Th.

————. Diaries. Five of Hagen's survive, dated 24 September 1844–18 December 1850; 1 July 1870–31 December 1870; 26 May 1877–4 June 1883; 13 June 1883–12 July 1886; and 15 July 1886–2 January 1888. All are in LMC Hagen.

————. *Die Gemeine Gottes, oder Die wahre Kirche Christi.* Lancaster, Pa.: Johann Bär's Söhnen, 1860. In an effort to respond to a pamphlet criticizing sects, Hagen defines the terms *congregation, church,* and *sect.* He completed his foreword 23 March 1860 in York, Pennsylvania.

————. "Eine Bitte aus Amerika an alle Brüdergemeinen." In *Der Brüder-Bote* 6, no. 1 (1867): 53. This is a plea in the form of a letter written from Bethlehem 16 November 1866 for funds to establish a mission to Germans living in New York City.

————. "In Memoriam, Sermon on the death of Rev. Edwin T. Senseman, who departed this life February 8, 1866, at Hope, Ind., preached in the Moravian Church on Staten Island, March 18th, 1866." Bethlehem, Pa.: Moravian Publication Office, 1866.

————. *The Moravian,* vol. 1, 1856, articles. "Reminiscences of the Moravian Church at York, Pa.," no. 1, 1 January 1856, p. 1. "Consecration of the Moravian Church in Philadelphia, Jan. 27th, 1856," no. 5, 1 February 1856, p. 33. "Visit to Graceham, Frederick Co., Maryland," no. 6, 8 February 1856, p. 42. "Lent," no. 8, 22 February 1856, p. 60. "Emmaus, Lehigh Co., Pa." (introduction to a report by John Regennas), no. 14, 4 April 1856, p. 105, "Confirmation", no. 14, 4 April 1856, p. 108. "Remarks on the above" (response to criticisms of Roepper), no. 14, 4 April 1856, p. 110. [Commentary on a report by Lewis Rights], no. 17, 25 April 1856, p. 129. [Response to commentary by German pastors], no. 22, 30 May 1856, p. 170. "The late southern Synod", no. 24, 13 June 1856, p. 185. "Confirmations, &c.," no. 25, 20 June 1856, p. 193. [Covering letter for a report by W. H. Van Vleck], no. 31, 1 August 1856, p. 243. "Our boarding schools", no. 35, 29 August 1856, p. 276. "Church music", no. 38, 19 September 1856, p. 300. "The coming provincial Synod," no. 39, 26 September 1856, p. 308. [Translation from Croeger], no. 46, 14 November 1856, p. 361;

no. 47, 21 November 1856, p. 369; no. 48, 28 November, p. 377. "Christmas," no. 52, 26 December 1856, p. 412. N.B. Anonymity was general in nineteenth-century periodicals. Contributions were generally partially anonymous, identified by initials or odd pseudonyms. Fortunately for our purposes, E. S. Hagen turned over to the Moravian Archives in Bethlehem a bound copy of Volume 1 in which contributors have been identified. A careful study of internal evidence provides other identifications.

C.	Clarke
F.	Kampmann
H.	Hagen
J. H.	James Henry
Mr. Moravian	Amadeus A. Reinke
R.	Roepper
E. T. S.	unidentified (historical matter)
Trennel	Lennert (spelled backwards)

————. (Memoir) "Mein Heiland. . . ." Translated by James Boeringer. Typescript in MMF Research Files, s.v. Hagen.

————. *Old Landmarks, or Faith and Practice of the Moravian Church at the Time of Its Revival and Restoration in 1727 and Twenty Years After.* Bethlehem, Pa., 1886. Hagen's source for this book is "Grosser Conferenz Syllabus," which, according to the listing in the Bethlehem Moravian Archives, is "a German manuscript containing minutes or extracts of minutes of the synods and synodal conferences from 1736 to 1745. According to a note on the wrapper in which this was received in 1960, this MS had once been in the possession of Peter Böhler." With this item are Hagen's manuscript translations, contained in eight volumes, extracts from which in turn became *Old Landmarks.* In his diary for November and December 1885, Hagen mentions reading proofs for this work.

————. "Pia desideria." In *The Moravian,* as follows. 1. 1/1, 1 January 1856, p. 5. 2. 1/2, 11 January 1856, p. 13. 3. 1/4, 25 January 1856, p. 29. 4. 1/6, 5 February 1856, p. 45. 5. 1/8, 22 February 1856, p. 61. 6. 1/12, 21 March 1856, p. 92. 7. 1/15, 11 April 1856, p. 117. 8. 1/18, 2 May 1856, p. 141. 9. 1/25, 20 June 1856, p. 194 (supplement: 1/43, 24 October 1856, p. 340). [Supplement to the series: "Sound doctrine," 1/27, 4 July 1856, p. 214.] 10. 11 July 1856, p. 221. 11. 1/33, 15 August 1856, p. 261. 12. 1/37, 12 September 1856, p. 292. 13. 1/41, 10 October 1856, p. 324. 14. 1/42, 17 October 1856, p. 334. 15. 1/49, 5 December 1856, p. 388.

————. *Rhymes on the Thirtieth of October, 1896, the 81st Birthday of the Rev. F. F. Hagen.* Pamphlet [1896]. Copy in MMF Research Files s.v. Hagen.

————. *Unitas Fratrum in Extremis; Thoughts on the Past and Present Condition of the Moravian Church in America, Respectfully Submitted to the Provincial Synod of 1893, at Bethlehem, Pa.* Bethlehem, Pa.: Moravian Publication Office, 1893. In a well-phrased and powerful essay, Hagen attacks the concept of the Moravian episcopacy and other high-church formalism and defends spontaneity and inward conversion.

Hagen, John Francis. Letter (27 December 1966) to Ewald V. Nolte. In MMF Research Files, s.v. Hagen.

————. "Some Memories of my Grandfather, Francis Florentine Hagen." Typescript copy in LMC Hagen.

Haupert, Raymond S. Letter (13 December 1965) to Ewald V. Nolte. In MMF Research Files, s.v. Hagen.

Mearns, James. "Scheffler, Johann (Angelus Silesius)." In Julian, John, *A Dictionary of Hymnology*. Rev. ed., with supplement. London, 1908, pp. 1004ff.

Mills, Mary Hagen (Mrs. Oscar E.). "Some memories of my grandfather, Francis Florentine Hagen." MMF Research Files, ms. s.v. Hagen.

New Dorp. Three autograph music notebooks with printed staves, the same shape as longways hymnals, with forty pages in each, containing eleven works, as follows. *I:* (1) "Kyrie eleison," p. 1, no. 35. (2) "Ye are come to Mt. Zion," p. 8, no. 80. (3) "And I heard a voice"—"Blessed are the dead," p. 24, no. 7. *II:* (1) "Lobsinget Gott," p. 1, no. 40. (2) *Christmas Carol*, p. 13. (3) "Hail, thou wondrous infant Stranger," p. 24, no. 27. (4) "Unto the Lamb," p. 25, no. 74. (5) Adagio "Songs of praise," p. 34. *III:* (1) "O delightful theme," p. 1, no. 49. (2) "Bis dereinst mein Stündlein schlägt," p. 12, no. 14. (3) "And the seventh angel," p. 25, no. 8. This is the first citation ever made of this source.

Pruett, James Worrell. "Francis Florentine Hagen, American Moravian Musician." Master's thesis, University of North Carolina, 1957. Copy at MMF, Peter Library.

Reichel, Th., comp. *Geburtstags-Buch mit Beigefügter Gemein-Chronik, herausgegeben im Jahr der General-Synod, 1857*. Leipzig, 1857. The particular copy cited contains inscriptions establishing that Edmund de Schweinitz in 1858 gave the book to Hagen, who in 1888 passed it on to Ernest. The family has continued to keep it up to date, and it is now in the possession of Mrs. Elizabeth Pfaff. Reichel cites the sources for his chronological information as Cröger's *Brüder Geschichte* (which Hagen later translated); the archives of the Unity at Kantzau; and *Gedenktage der Erneuerten Brüderkirche*.

Reinke, S. "Zum Jubel- Geburtstags-Fest meines herzlich geliebten Freundes & Bruders, Franz Florentin Hagen, Bethlehem, den 30ten October, 1865." Typescript in MMF Research Files, s.v. Hagen. This remarkable gesture of friendship consists of fifty quatrains, one for each year of Hagen's life.

Répertoire international des sources musicales (RISM), Einzeldrucke vor 1800. Kassel, 1981, s.v. Hagen, Vanderhagen, etc.

Steelman, Robert. *Catalog of the Lititz Congregation Collection.* Chapel Hill, 1981, 230.1, "Morning Star," no. 44; 344.2, "Sel'ge Lebensstunden," no. 61; 377.1, "Morning Star," no. 44.

Transactions of the Moravian Historical Society, vol. 13, p. 59. Obituary of F. F. Hagen.

Wolfe, Richard J. *Secular music in America, 1801–1825, A Bibliography.* New York, 1964, s.v. Hagen.

Zahn, Johannes. *Die Melodien der deutschen evangelischen Kirchenlieder, aus den Quellen geschöpft und mitgeteilt.* Gütersloh, 1889. As cited in detail in Appendix 3.